There's No Time Like Today
To Look and Feel
Alive and Well and Better Than Ever!

If you have picked up this book, then you care about yourself. You care how you look, how you feel, and how others think of you. You may not know it, but you've already begun the marvelous *Alive & Well*® program of health and beauty for women over forty.

Now, all you need to do is take the next step—follow the plan, have fun with it, and reap the exciting results. Take a little time every day to care about yourself— that's the secret of success. The results will be stunningly clear to you and everyone in just a few short, energizing weeks.

ALIVE & WELL AND OVER FORTY®

IT CAN BE YOU.

Other Bantam Books in the *Alive & Well* Series
Ask your bookseller for the books you have missed

ALIVE & WELL NATURALLY®

ALIVE & WELL AND OVER 40®

Kay Sullivan

BANTAM BOOKS
TORONTO · NEW YORK · LONDON · SYDNEY

ALIVE & WELL AND OVER 40®
A Bantam Book / May 1984

ISBN 0-553-24107-9

Published simultaneously in the United States and Canada

Bantam Books are published by Bantam Books, Inc. Its trademark, consisting of the words "Bantam Books" and the por-
trayal of a rooster, is Registered in U.S. Patent and Trademark
Office and in other countries. Marca Registrada. Bantam
Books, Inc., 666 Fifth Avenue, New York, New York 10103.

PRINTED IN THE UNITED STATES OF AMERICA

H   0 9 8 7 6 5 4 3 2 1

*To Susan S. Anderson and Gail S. Rand
for their loving support.*

Acknowledgments

One of the nice things about writing a health and beauty book is the fact that there are always experts at hand happy to share their knowledge with you. My interviews with Dr. Albert Kligman of the University of Pennsylvania Medical School on skin and sun, Phyllis Klein of Clairol on hair and hair color, Annette Green of the Fragrance Foundation on perfume usage, Dr. Deborah T. Sharpe on fashion color choices and Pablo Manzoni on makeup techniques are instances of such cooperation.

There were many more, too numerous to list here. And for their generous assistance, I would also thank the American Medical Association, the American Academy of Dermatology, the American Academy of Facial Plastic and Reconstruction Surgery, the National Hairdressers and Cosmetologists Association, the Department of Health and Human Services, Food and Drug Administration and the Metropolitan Life Insurance Company.

Contents

FOREWORD   xiii

1   YOUNGER IS UP   1

Standing up straight may be something you think schoolchildren should be told, but try it for yourself and discover what an effective beauty treatment it can be.

2   YOU CAN'T KNOW TOO MUCH ABOUT SKIN   8

Skin is a tattletale. If you haven't been taking proper care of yours, it could be spreading bad news. But it's never too late to improve on the performance and appearance of your skin. Here's what you can do.

3   HOW TO STEP ON A CROW'S FOOT   19

You'll definitely be encouraged by this discussion of aging skin problems, including wrinkles, creases, crepey eyelids, and liver spots, plus a look at that biggest skin threat of all, the suntan.

4   HAPPY WITH YOUR HAIR?   30

Did you ever realize what a few streaks of sunshine in your hair could do for your appearance? All about hair color and the latest hair coloring techniques, plus some fascinating news about perms.

5 SORTING OUT TOP PROBLEMS 38

How would you describe your hair condition? Baby fine, oily, too curly, coarse, dull, dry, brittle, or dandruff-y? If you've got a problem, here are some very helpful answers.

6 THE MAGIC OF MAKEUP 46

Come right in to our makeup class and get a step-by-step lesson that will show you how to apply your makeup so that it's outrageously flattering. Also, are you getting and giving a message via perfume?

7 THE BEAUTY BATH AND MORE 59

You can take a bath or shower merely to get clean, or you can turn either one into a refreshing, rejuvenating beauty experience. Here's how, along with some advice on superfluous hair, deodorants, and depilatories.

8 HELP FOR YOUR HANDS AND FEET 69

Ever say to yourself, "I like wearing gloves—they cover up my old-looking hands"? Or, "My feet are killing me"? Read this chapter and you'll never utter those words again.

9 WINNING THE DIET GAME 82

You cannot lose weight if you really don't want to. Get yourself the proper motivation, apply these provocative, commonsense ideas about the food you eat—then step on the scales and celebrate.

10 BODY SHAPING 90

Too old to exercise? Never. Your problem may be that you think calisthenics are the only way to exercise. Find out about other ways to trim your figure and have fun doing them.

11 HOW YOUNG IS YOUR PERSONALITY? 104

Bodies age; personalities don't have to. Some thoughts about the image you are projecting and how to make your movements say "young" instead of "old."

12 THE WAY YOU DRESS—GOOD, BAD,
OR INDIFFERENT   114

How to figure out your figure type and choose
clothes to flatter it. What color can do for you, and
why you should never sell accessories short.

13 WHAT'S NEW IN PLASTIC SURGERY   128

You're probably well aware of the popularity of
face-lifts and eye tucks but have you heard about
plastic surgery for jodhpur thighs and saddlebag hips?
Here's a review of developments in the world of
cosmetic surgery plus some guidelines on finding
the right plastic surgeon for your needs.

14 YOUR PERSONAL BEAUTY AND
HEALTH PLAN   138

A summary of tips for making the most of your
looks, your figure, your clothes, and your personality.

Foreword

How long has it been since you studied your complexion in a magnifying mirror? Or stepped out of the tub or shower and looked at your figure in a full-length mirror? (That's sideways as well as a front view.) Or studied your feet before pulling on your hose? Or peered at the way your hair looks in back? Or given yourself a careful manicure instead of dabbing new polish on top of old? Or weighed yourself and admitted the scale was correct, not broken.

Now don't stop reading. This beauty book is not intended to be a lecture. We are not going to scold you. Well, hardly. Let's say instead that we want to raise your "self-consciousness level." We'd like to help you become aware of exactly how you look to other people. If you discover that there are things about your appearance that you don't like or that you wish could be changed, we're going to offer you advice so that you can make positive changes.

Although we specifically plan to address mature women, aged forty or more, *every* woman can benefit by the advice and information in these pages. The questions in the opening paragraph of this foreword can be just as meaningful to a teenager as they might be to her older sister, mother, or aunt.

No matter how attractive a woman is, there always is room for improvement. Most young women appreciate this fact. They seldom seem to be satisfied with the way they look. Let some new cosmetic product arrive on the market and they rush to buy it. They're the ones who try the latest lipstick, blusher, or perfume. They're born experimenters, constantly switching shampoos, conditioners, hairstyles, and even their hair color. And totally unfazed by rapidly changing fashion trends. Whatever's "in" is what they're wearing.

Mature women tend to avoid the flurry and furor about what's new. They're more apt to fall into the "comfortable" trap. They find it easier and more comfortable to stay with the same old hairstyle. Safer to stick to the same shade of lipstick—after all, it matches last season's wardrobe perfectly. Besides, a different shade of lipstick might mean a new blusher.

Ask the mature woman if she'd like to change her perfume and she's apt to ask why. After all, she was wearing it at the Senior Prom when she met George. (What she doesn't realize is that she and George have been smelling that same floral scent for so long that it has lost its magical impact. In fact, George thinks it's soap.)

If you are a mature woman who is interested—no, anxious—to improve your appearance, there are certain things that are vital for you to do. First, you must develop a total awareness of the way you look now and the way you could look. That's why we asked those nosy questions at the outset—we're hoping to prod you into honestly evaluating your appearance. Too many women see only what they want to see when they look at themselves in a mirror. Or they conveniently ignore the obvious. You know the type: The woman who brags about her unlined complexion but doesn't seem to know there's a lot of dark fuzz on her upper lip.

The second requirement in your self-improvement program is possibly less painful than the first. It's merely to renew your knowledge of your body, the way it functions, and the way it ages. Learn more about your skin, its complexities, what it does for you, and what threatens it. Find out how to analyze your hair so that you can understand why it is limp or oily or frizzy . . . or just perfect. Read up on nutrition, diet, and exercise. The more knowledge you gain in these areas, the better able you'll be to make improvements.

And your third order of the day? Be adventurous.

One of the chief reasons why you're bored with the way you look now probably is because you haven't done any experimenting with new beauty products, with new makeup techniques, or with your clothes. For example, are you using a blow dryer to style your hair? Or lip gloss in place of lipstick? Is your constant uniform a tailored blouse with a skirt or pants plus flats? Or have you tried some of the new dramatic, voluminous styles and higher heels? (And don't say you seldom wear dresses because of the veins on your legs. All it takes to make those unattractive veins practically invisible is five extra minutes in the morning with some cover-up makeup a shade darker than your skin tone.)

Now that lends us right to a fourth "must" which should be added to the trio of rules just reviewed. Take time for beauty. Take time for a leisurely bath, for a thorough shampoo and conditioning of your hair, and for a manicure and pedicure. Take time to remove your makeup and cleanse your skin thoroughly. Take time to apply your makeup artfully. Continue on the same slapdash pattern of beauty care you've been following, and you're not going to see much change in your appearance.

The next time you notice a stunning face on a magazine cover, just consider the fact that the model arrived at the photographer's studio at nine o'clock in the morning and spent until noon preparing for that cover shot. We're not suggesting that you spend three hours applying your makeup and arranging your hair, but why not allow just a little more time each day for grooming? If you slept on your hair the wrong way and some ends are sticking out like spikes, take time to coax them back into place with pin curls and hair spray. Or reach for your curling iron. It won't take long. It takes only a little more time than usual to carefully work your mascara out to the very ends of your eyelashes—but your eyes are going to look far more eloquent. And you only need to spend a moment more to outline your lips before applying your lipstick. But your lips will look shapelier and much more appealing.

So there it is—just fours steps to take for the New You.

- Know what you look like right now...and consider some changes.
- Renew and update your knowledge of the body and its workings.
- Resolve to be more adventurous about beauty products, beauty treatments and techniques, and fragrances and fashions.
- Stop rushing—give yourself more time for personal care, for your skin and hair, for your figure, and for your wardrobe.

Makeovers at any age are not easily accomplished. They take patience, time, and know-how. But along the way you can count on them to be exciting and surprising. And eventually, rewarding.

No Time Like Right Now

Possibly the nicest thing about trying to look younger and prettier is the fact that you can't lose if you go about it properly. And there's no need to feel self-conscious about your efforts. A desire for beauty is far from superficial or selfish. Rather, it's an indication of your sensitivity of mind and spirit and your awareness of those around you.

No matter how badly you may have neglected yourself during the salad years, the dessert years can still be beautiful. You have lots of options—marvelous, workable ways and means to recapture a vital, vivacious look, coax a gleam back into dull hair, brighten a drab complexion, and streamline a spreading silhouette.

The head of a famous model agency once said, "It's perfectly possible for any woman to give the illusion of youth and beauty—all she needs are an appealing personality and one or two attractive features."

You simply dramatize the attractive features, allowing the rest of you to be the "supporting cast." And you surround the entire production with that appealing personality.

That's the whole secret—and now *you* know it.

1/ Younger Is Up

Don't tell us—we know. You've reached a plateau in your life when you think it really doesn't matter how you look. You are happily married. You have a wonderful family life. You are surrounded by loving friends. You have a successful career. But there were forty candles on your last birthday cake and you've been telling yourself ever since that it's perfectly natural to have a double chin, a droopy bustline, and a few extra pounds on each hip. And quite likely you have a lot of support for your attitude. A great many of your women friends feel the same way. It's a kind of "Why do I have to prove anything anymore?" mentality that condones "taking it easy." But taking it easy about your looks is a gigantic mistake. Just ask the next dermatologist or hairstylist you meet. Or diet or exercise expert. Or makeup artist or fashion designer. Or even your doctor. Especially your doctor. They'll all tell you that things get progressively worse when neglected.

Making the absolute most of your appearance is a lifetime battle but because it's *your* battle, you can't afford to lose. If you've given up and retired from the front lines, get yourself back in the fray. You've got the potential needed to win. But before you make a move,

1

you should evaluate your equipment. And overhaul your attitude. Think young and you'll find yourself acting, feeling, and looking young. Keep nursing grim thoughts about getting old and you may soon qualify as a genuine antique.

There are many ways you can launch a "look younger and prettier" campaign: Spend a week at a spa; change your hair color; join an exercise class; or give yourself a facial. Eventually, we hope you'll try all of them but we would suggest a good way to begin is to get "uppity." And you can take that literally. "Upness" is to the business of looking young what soft music is to romance. The younger-looking a woman remains, the more apt she is to keep her head up, chin up, and chest us. And no doubt, the corners of her mouth. And knowing what it does to ward off age-making varicose veins, she probably puts her feet up whenever possible.

What we're really talking about is good posture—standing up straight. If you aren't doing it, you're adding years to your appearance. Neck, chin, waistline and stomach, hips, and legs are all affected for better or worse by your posture. If it's good, your figure looks good. If it's bad, you could have the curviest shape this side of Hollywood and still look terrible. Bad posture adds up to bulges, sags and slumps, aches and pains, tension, and a tired expression.

Unfortunately, bad posture, like all bad habits, is easy to acquire, but difficult to lose. It's going to take daily concentration on your part to correct your stance but it will be worthwhile. Good posture is the quickest beauty treatment available and the one that shows the most dramatic results.

An easy way to determine whether or not you're holding yourself properly erect is to place your back to a wall, your feet a few inches from it. If your posture is close to perfect, your head, shoulders, and buttocks will be touching the wall and the small of your back will be no more than a hand's thickness away from it.

The rules for good posture may sound complicated but it's really not hard to achieve. In fact, if you practice it for any length of time, you'll find going back to your old slump or slouch can be actually painful. Think of posture as a kind of body sculpture with yourself as the artist or sculptor. It's up to you to make those body lines beautiful, whether you're standing, moving, or sitting.

Stretch your body upward and hold it comfortably—not stiffly—erect, with your weight evenly distributed on both feet. Your head should "sit" directly on your spine as though you were suspended by the tips of your ears. Hold the back of your neck straight, your chin parallel to the floor. Keep your shoulders down and slightly back and your chest lifted. Buttock muscles should be slightly contracted; stomach muscles taut. Let your knees flex slightly.

Now take a look at your reflection in the mirror (we hope you're wearing a minimum of clothes for this test—no peplums or pleats to blur your improved silhouette). The first thing you'll notice is that your midriff looks inches thinner. That's why good posture is labeled "instant weight loss." And notice too how much more confident, graceful, and poised you look.

Of course if you're twenty pounds overweight, just assuming good posture is not going to obliterate all the bulges that blur your body line. Nonetheless, you should feel better about yourself. Certainly you'll feel "taller." Your chin, throat, and shoulder lines will be much improved. Keep working at good posture; coupled with diet and exercise, it will definitely make a radical change in your appearance. And you can use a little extra help to keep those abdominal muscles taut. Panty hose with a firm girdle top or panty briefs of sturdy stretch fabric can do a lot toward keeping a stomach curve going in instead of out. And a properly fitted uplift or longline bra can help firm and shape your top half.

But just one test session in front of a mirror isn't

going to guarantee anyone that forever more she'll stand beautifully balanced. You're probably going to have to trick yourself into remembering to practice good posture and here's a thought about that. Paste a tiny circle of paper with the word *Up* on it on your watch dial. Then, whenever you want to see what time it is, you'll be reminded. Keep thinking your body "up" whether standing, walking, or sitting. Push your head up, up, up as though you were trying to bump into the sky, or at least, a ceiling. You'll feel your neck lengthening (there go the accordion pleats in it), your bosom rising, your waist slimming, and your stomach flattening. And you thought good posture was a bore! Instead, it's a bonus, to be applied to your look-younger account.

The Way You Walk and Sit

Correct posture isn't just for standing; it affects the way you walk and the way you sit. If you're in the habit of walking with your shoulders hunched and your head thrust forward, you're not going to win any awards for youthful grace. But with good posture, it should be easy for you to develop a rhythmic stride and springy step that says "young."

The ground rules for graceful walking, as taught to models, go thus: As you walk, your heels should follow a straight line and your toes should point out slightly. Let the heel of the foot touch the floor first, then the ball and the toe. Keep your knees slightly flexed; they absorb the shock of walking. But walk from the hips—as though your legs swing out from somewhere just beneath your ribs. Your arms should be relaxed and swing freely from your shoulders but never in an exaggerated windmill fashion. Don't waddle and don't sway your hips from side to side. Waddling is the lazy way to walk—it's walking from the knees down instead of striding easily from the hips. As for swaying, every time you move your hips back and forth, you're wasting energy. Use your muscles to propel your body forward, not sideways.

The way you sit in a chair can make you appear poised and confident or fidgety and uncertain. A child can flop down in a chair, legs apart, arms dangling, and get away with it. A woman, especially if she's overweight and heavy-thighed, risks looking grotesque. To sit attractively, lower yourself into a chair with all the fluid grace you can muster. Keep your bottom pressed against the back of the chair, the weight of your thighs evenly distributed on the seat. (If you sit forward on the edge of a chair, your thighs bear the weight of your entire body. Do this all day long—in the office, for example—and you wind up with flabby thighs.) Hold your shoulders back slightly; keep your backbone upright in its natural line, keep your head erect, and rest your feet flat on the floor.

As you sit, if you can't fit both hands flat, one above the other, between your bosom and your waist, you're slumping. (Check right now to see if you're guilty.)

There's an art to crossing your legs, too. For a graceful, pretty line, cross your right leg over the left, then move your legs slightly to the left. Or reverse. The same goes for crossing ankles. Right ankle over left, then move legs to the right for a fluid line. Or reverse. Naturally, if your legs are your good point, cross them by all means. It will help call attention to them. But forget crossing your legs or ankles if you have very heavy legs or short legs. No need to focus on a flaw.

Up with Your Feet

We mentioned earlier that keeping your feet elevated is a good way to help avert the development of varicose veins and keep legs looking younger. That's not all a feet-up policy can do for you. Try it to improve your complexion.

An abundant supply of blood and oxygen to the head is crucial for healthy good looks. Without adequate oxygen, the skin begins to sag, the eyes lose their sparkle, and the hair becomes straggly and dull. But put your body on an upslant and blood will flush into your face and neck. Oxygen will circulate throughout your body and help burn up waste and throw off dead cells. White corpuscles will move in to do their good work and food and minerals will be carried along in the bloodstream to help rebuild cell tissue.

Some health experts recommend standing on your head to achieve this all-important beauty flush. But for those of us who are not too well-balanced, there's an easier solution. You can buy a professional slant board to tilt the body up at the proper angle. Or you can improvise with an ironing board. Make sure it's fixed firmly in place against a chair, then stretch out on it, feet elevated fifteen inches above your head. As pressure is removed from the legs and the lower part of the body, and blood flows to the face and scalp, your entire circulation will be stimulated in a healthy fashion. Three minutes a day in this feet-up position is relaxing; ten minutes is reviving, and twenty minutes a day could mean you'll never need a face-lift. Every time you do the Feet-Up Slant, you're fighting off the inroads of age a little bit more. Try it when you give yourself a facial or put on your nail polish. Or when you're telephoning a garrulous friend. Don't worry about the ironing: Maintaining a youthful glow is much more important.

Keep Your Chin Up

When a chin is single, it gets very little attention. But just let it double and you get the feeling that the whole world is looking at it. More than anything else, the solution for a double chin is upness. It's almost impossible for a well-lifted chin to multiply. If your body is perfectly aligned, your chin should lift automatically. And the jowliness and little "squirrel pockets" that usually go with double chins, vanish.

The best friend a double chin ever had is a big, plump pillow. Sleeping without a pillow is much better for your chinline. If you simply can't do without one, at least use a pillow that is reasonably thin and firm, or a "barbell" pillow—the type that supports your neck and head without pushing your chin forward.

Cosmetically, stimulation and massage can help restore tautness to a wayward chin. Take advantage of astringents, facial masks, and contour preparations, plus massage to help firm up those relaxed lines, rev up circulation, and break down the fatty accumulations present under the chin.

An effective antidouble chin exercise goes like this: Sit tall in front of a mirror. Push your chin forward as far as it will go. Then push your lower lip forward. Remaining in this position, turn your head very slowly to the left, then very slowly to the right. You'll feel those throat and jaw muscles tighten. Do ten to fifteen times frequently.

Remember, a double chin is not necessarily a sign of age—but it is a sure indication that something is wrong with one's posture. Think chin, think up!

2 / You Can't Know Too Much about Skin

Skin is an outrageous tattletale. Get angry and it turns red. Become frightened and it blanches. Grow embarrassed and it blushes. And it can be the first thing to betray a woman's age. You've probably seen how it does this all too often.

Standing in line at a bank or supermarket, you admire the woman ahead of you. Not a gray hair on her head; figure trim as a teenager's; clothes incredibly chic. Then she turns and you get your first glimpse of her face—leathery, crisscrossed with fine lines, sunken here, and sagging there. It's like that famous scene from *Lost Horizon* all over again, when the heroine turns instantly from a fresh-faced beauty into a wrinkled crone.

Or you go to your college reunion and encounter a former roommate, the one who was voted the class beauty. One look at her multiple crow's feet, crepey eyelids, creases around her mouth, and brown spots on her skin, and you skip the dean's dinner and rush home to look in a mirror. And to think she is only a year younger than you!

What you must remember constantly is that skin is sensitive—almost too sensitive. Everything seems to affect it. Your age does. So does the climate where you live. Exposure to the elements can toughen it. Friction and pressure can increase its thickness. Warmth relaxes it; cold contracts it. And you can expect the texture of skin to change somewhat whenever you lose sleep, take certain medications, or make a drastic change in your diet. Go on a trip, adopt a new life-style, become nervous and tense for some reason, and believe it or not, your skin reacts. In other words, your skin, the mirror, reflects whatever you're up to. Or not up to, as regards proper cleansing and care.

Neglect and/or improper care have ruined many a dewy complexion. And then there are certain inevitable physical changes to do it harm as time goes by. You can count on fine lines and little wrinkles to appear sometime after you've reached thirty-plus. (Look for them on the neck—that's their port of entry. Their first landing place on the face is that delicate eyelid skin.) Body metabolism begins to slow down, affecting the way skin cells behave and reducing the blood supply to the skin's surface. Supportive tissue beneath the skin's surface starts to weaken. Melanin or pigment cells lose their sense of direction, accumulating in some areas, diminishing in others. All this can mean that you wind up without your youthful plump, glowing complexion and with a lot of crisscrossy lines plus a mottled look in its place.

Happily you do have a weapon against wrinkles, crinkles, and creases—moisturizing. Skin is about seventy-percent water, with the outer layer about ten-percent. most of the water in this outer layer comes from within the body; you add a small amount from the outside every time you bathe or wash your face. But water evaporates quickly from the skin's surface. That's where those natural oils in your skin come into play; they act as a barrier to keep the water from disappearing completely. Or you help things along by slathering a moisturizer on your skin.

Just what is a moisturizer? Simply a mix of oil and water. Apply one to your face or body and the water softens and plumps up the skin cells; the oils form a barrier against evaporation and help make your skin feel smooth. In the meanwhile, those newly plumped-up skin cells hide the tiny lines that are making your skin look old. (Incidentally, the best time to apply any moisturizer is right after you have washed your skin; it will lock in any of the dampness still clinging to it.

Your Skin, Your Friend

Even though you may get upset with your skin now and then for looking less than its best, you must admit it's a fantastic possession. Not just because it's a vital organ of your body and the only one instantly visible and conveniently available for care and control. But because it does so much for you. It's a flexible wrapper, protecting your bones, muscles, and body tissues. It's a health warden, throwing off water and mineral wastes, holding back the onslaughts of bacteria. It shelters nerves, blood vessels, and fat glands and provides a base for those important hair follicles. (The sebaceous glands at the root of those follicles make and distribute the vital oils that maintain the skin's suppleness and lend sheen to both skin and hair.) It's your personal, built-in air conditioner, helping to regulate body temperature and preventing dehydration.

Yet another admirable quality about skin is the way it renews itself. Just about every twenty-seven days you get a whole new skin. That's the life span of your epidermal or surface cells that are washed or rubbed away. (Mostly, they flake off in the night when you're sleeping.)

Also, skin repairs itself nobly. Cut, scrape, or burn

it in the sun, and it will heal, although not always in the same way and in the identical length of time. Black skin and Oriental skin, thicker than Caucasian skin, tend to heal more slowly and show keloids or scar tissue. On the other hand, Caucasian skin burns and peels more readily when exposed indiscriminately to the sun's ultraviolet rays.

Layers upon Layers

Ordinarily, you probably don't think about the make-up of your skin but just the makeup you rub, brush, and pat on it. But something so complex in character deserves contemplation once in a while.

There's the epidermis or outer layer, the one you cleanse, moisturize, and adorn with cosmetics. Actually, it consists of several layers but the one that concerns you the most is the basal layer. The cells in this layer are continually dividing to renew the life of your skin. The new cells stay below for a time to carry on their vital work; the old ones rise to the surface where they are gradually sloughed off. The epidermis also contains those important melanin cells, the ones that carry the pigment that gives your skin its color.

Below the epidermis is the dermis, an elastic, pliable tissue containing a rich supply of nerves and blood vessels that carry nourishment to the skin. The dermis is made up of a protein fiber that accounts for most of your skin's elasticity. Once those elastic fibers and other dermal cellular elements like collagen are weakened by age, the skin loses its capacity to stretch and bounce back. The dermis also houses hair follicles, and oil and sweat glands.

Finally, there's the subdermis, consisting mainly of fatty tissue; it does vital, although undramatic, work.

By the way, the next time you catch yourself saying, "I just about jumped out of my skin," know that you'd be leaving behind about seven pounds. That's what scientists have estimated a woman's skin usually weighs. (It's ten pounds for men.) While they were at it, they also determined that your skin covers an average area of some nineteen square feet.

And don't ever claim to being totally thin-skinned—or thick-skinned, for that matter. Skin varies in thickness on everyone, ranging from 1/50th to 1/8th of an inch. Thinnest on the face, neck, and eyelids; thickest on the palms of the hands, the soles of the feet, and the back. (If you happen to have a pregnant friend, reassure her with the news that skin is most stretchable on the abdomen.)

What Type Are You?

Before you can do right by your skin, you have to know its type—normal, oily, dry, or a combination. You can test your skin yourself, or better still, consult a skin care expert. And don't think you already know your skin type because a cosmetician told you when you were in high school. Skin types change frequently, particularly as you grow older.

When testing your skin, do so early in the morning. That gives your skin all night to establish its true personality. Use strips of oil-blotting tissue that you can get at any drugstore or just ordinary tissue paper, the kind you use for gift-wrapping. Press a strip lightly on your forehead, chin, nose, and cheek. If you skin is normal, the tissues will stick to your face but show no oily patches. If your skin is oily, the tissues will stick readily and oily patches will be quite apparent on the paper. If your skin is dry, the strips will barely stick or fall off and nothing will show on them.

Briefly, here are descriptions of the various skin types and tips about caring for them.

NORMAL

This is the skin every woman would love to have—
fresh, firm, fine-grained, supple, and smooth-textured.
Pores are practically invisible; blemishes almost unheard-
of. With a skin this perfect, the danger is that you take it
for granted. You may treat it too casually, scrub it too
hard, or forget to moisturize it regularly. After age thirty,
normal skin develops a tendency to dryness. If you use
soap and water for cleansing, make it a mild soap and
be sure to rinse thoroughly. If you use cleansing creams
or lotions to remove makeup, use a mild skin freshener
afterward to keep pores clear. At night, after cleansing,
apply a lubricating cream or lotion. Always use a light
moisturizer under makeup and protect your skin with a
sunscreen whenever you spend time in the sun.

DRY

No one has to tell you about dry skin if you have it.
You know how it feels—uncomfortable more often than
not. Dry skin chaps and flakes easily; feels taut in cold
weather and especially after soap and water washings.
You never have to worry about a shiny nose—your skin
doesn't have much natural oil. It also lacks elasticity.
That, plus those underactive oil glands and your skin's
inability to retain much moisture, means early wrinkling,
especially around the eye and mouth areas. Give your
thirsty skin all the moisturizing you can, day and night.
Avoid soap and water scrubbings; wash gently, using a
mild glycerin or superfatted soap. Or emollient cleansing creams and lotions. No astringents for you; just skin
fresheners without an alcohol base. Night creams and
eye creams are musts; so are sunscreens, cold-weather
protection, body lotions, and bath oils. Drink several
glasses of water each day. If the water where you live is
hard, a water softener would be a wise investment for

you. So would a humidifier for winter weather when artificial heat robs humidity from the indoors air. If you're going to be in the sun, always use a sunscreen; pick one with an oil base.

OILY

This is the skin type that calls for firm discipline; it's the skin with the perpetual shine; the one that always seems to feel sticky and that is no stranger to large pores and blemishes. Take heart: When skin that is either normal or dry is showing its age, the oily skin stays young and supple. Your big challenge is to keep your skin free of excess oiliness but this doesn't mean you should strip away every last bit of oil. Warm water, neutral or medicated soaps, and antibacterial cleansing lotions are your good friends. Thorough cleansings and careful makeup removal are absolute musts. Wipe off cleansing creams quickly: don't let them linger. Follow up with a skin freshener and apply an astringent where pores are the largest. Weekly facials will help keep your skin looking brighter and fresher.

COMBINATION

Combination skin has a firm, smooth texture and looks healthy but alas, all is not perfection. There's a constant sheen on the forehead and around the nose and mouth. But cheeks, jawline, and the outer edges of the forehead tend to be dry and flaky. Sometimes, large pores and blemishes show up around the nose and chin. You've got the skin that calls for more specialized attention than any other. You must treat the two problem areas differently, using dry skin preparations on the arid areas; an oily skin routine on the T-zone. Don't think it's impossible to wash just the oily parts of your face; it's not. Lather your forehead, nose, and chin with a medicated soap and then rinse well, pouring the water from your cupped hands or from a glass to keep it concentrated in the right areas. Finish by using an astringent to tighten the T-zone pores. Tackle the dry areas of your face with a cleansing cream or lotion: follow with a nondrying toner or freshener. Pay close attention to your throat and the area around your eyes, keeping a light moisturizing cream on during the day; a richer emollient cream at night.

The Right Way to Handle Your Skin

As you get older and your skin gets thinner, you must pamper it more; handle it carefully. Pulling, stretching, and pressing heavily on it can actually damage it. The key word is *gently*. Don't ever draw facial skin downward; use upward, outward movements when applying creams, lotions, cream foundations, and blushers.

You can use a fairly firm, circular motion on the forehead, nose, and chin because the skin here is supported by the bone structure beneath. At the hairline, too, you can use a rotary motion that is firm and stimulating. But never pull down on the throat skin or stretch it from side to side. Starting from the collarbone, use a hand-over-hand movement, upward and out when applying moisturizers and creams.

If directions read "patting the skin," it doesn't mean pressing your fingers deep into the flesh, but touching it lightly with the fingertips. (When patting around cheeks and lips, always puff them out. It's easier to do a better job with a little resistance from within.) When you come to the eye area, stroke it gently with the pads of the fingers, moving from the inside corner of the eye outward and upward to the brow. Be especially careful not to stretch the skin on your eyelids and around the eyes when you remove eyeshadow and mascara. This is crinkle territory; don't make it even more apparent.

Any kind of extreme pressure on sensitive, older

skin is bad for it. For example, if you have a habit of resting your head on your hands, make sure that you're not pushing your fist into your cheek. Try resting one arm across your midriff, then use it to support the elbow of your other arm. Prop your chin on the back of your hand—that way, there's no undue pressure on facial skin.

Taking proper care of your skin is one beauty proposition that never stops paying dividends. Skin-care routines don't have to be complicated. All that really is required is to know your own skin and the specific treatment that will do the most for it. Use only the products that are especially designed for your type of skin—and use them regularly. Now and then isn't enough when you're out to make improvements.

On with the Mask

A mask is a kind of exercise for your complexion. No matter what type of skin you have, masks can be beneficial. They activate circulation, soften lines, loosen and remove impurities, and in general, refresh and revitalize your complexion. There literally are dozens of masks on the market—cleansing, deep-cleansing, moisturizing, all-purpose, exfoliating, stimulating, rinse-off, and peel-off. Masks contain workaday ingredients like mud; others count on exotic contents like honey and fruit to work wonders with your skin.

You should select a mask according to your skin type. One designed for an oily skin, for example, would be too drying for a sensitive skin. Likewise, the frequency with which you use masks should relate directly to your skin type. Some can be used every day or several times a week; others less often.

You can maximize the effects of a mask by first steaming your face to dissolve oil-clogging pores and to provide the skin with valuable moisture. Or if you are not planning on using a mask, take time to cleanse your face using a gentle mist. It's an excellent way of refreshing and toning your skin. You may want to use an appliance especially designed for this kind of gentle misting. Or with a towel draped over your head and shoulders in tent-fashion, bend over a large bowl or sink full of hot water. Steam for about ten minutes. Keep your face at least a foot from the water and come up for air occasionally. Then blot your face gently and see how thoroughly clean and fresh your skin feels.

Cleansing your face with a gentle mist opens up pores in preparation for the good work a mask can do. It is especially helpful in advance of a cleansing mask because it helps the mask get through to the skin more effectively.

Brush-on, peel-off masks are especially good for combination and oily skins. Dab or brush them on and feel your skin tingle as they tighten up. Once dry, peel off (if you can do it in one piece, give yourself an award). With it will come dry, dead skin, and dirt and oily impurities. Cleansing masks do a thorough job of getting skin clean and usually can be identified by a slightly grainy texture or mudlike consistency. Deep-cleansing masks exfoliate the dead top layers of skin. Moisturizing masks cleanse and add moisturizer to the skin at the same time—ideal for the dry complexion. Look for astringent and medicated masks, too. Recommended for oily skins, they temporarily dry the skin and make pores less apparent. Some are medicated.

Whatever your choice of mask, apply it carefully, stroking it onto your face, over your forehead, nose, and chin, and from cheeks back to the ears. Keep it away from eye and lip areas where tender skin could become too dry.

Lie down, close your eyes, and relax for ten minutes or whatever the specified time in the mask instructions. You may want to keep your eyes covered with an eye mask or cotton pads soaked in witch hazel or an astringent. When it's time to remove the mask, rinse your face generously with warm water, then cold. A moist sponge will help clear away a hardened mask. Finish up with a skin freshener and eye cream. Your pores will be tightened, your skin aglow, and your complexion feeling and looking fresh and radiant.

3 / How to Step on a Crow's Foot

There are few shocks in life to equal the discovery of your first wrinkle. It's like finding out that your best friend voted against you for the presidency of the Garden Club. Or that the alligator pumps you paid a small fortune for are actually processed vinyl. A first wrinkle rates tearful concern for at least a full week. The second, third, and all subsequent wrinkles go unrecognized. It's been said that the twenty-year-old ignores them; the thirty-year-old buries them under makeup; and the forty-year-old says, "What's the use?"

But whether they're noticed or not, most wrinkles are encouraged to settle in, thanks to inadequate or improper skin care and poor facial habits. If you're too tired at bedtime to remove the top of a jar of nourishing skin cream and apply as directed, you're going to have to lie there and let the wrinkles deepen. And if you insist on punctuating everything you say or do with a wince, a squint, or a frown, be prepared. Those creases are going to show up as fast and as frequently as chase scenes on TV thrillers.

Add weather to your natural tendencies toward

sloth and grimacing, and you can understand why you're wrinkle-prone. Icy breezes in the winter, hot sun in the summer, plus overheated and overair-conditioned homes and offices—they're all first-class wrinkle-makers.

Naturally, time is no help at all in the battle of the crow's foot. It marches on, bringing with it first the crepey eyelids and the crow's feet at the lateral angles of the eyes. Then the furrows on the forehead and the so-called laugh lines around the nose and mouth. Then the network of lines on the cheeks. And those little vertical creases above the upper lip, just reposing there waiting to trap lipstick in their ridges.

It's grim reality—but not for everyone. Some lucky faces will never know what it's like to be laced with lines. The tendency to develop wrinkles—or conversely, to retain a youthful-looking, wrinkle-free skin is inherited. So, if you have a relatively wrinkle-free skin, thank past relatives.

Even in this enlightened age, there is nothing you can apply to the skin or take orally to prevent wrinkles. But you can retard their appearance and once they make their debut, you can lull them into looking less dramatic than the Grand Canyon. Your best weapon in the struggle is moisturizing. You read in the previous chapter how important it is to keep the skin constantly moisturized. A moisturizer creates a protective surface film over the skin that slows down water evaporation loss from the epidermis and shields it from environmental rigors. It's difficult for skin to crinkle up when it's soft and moist. It makes good sense to keep some kind of moisturizer on your face around the clock.

Another good-sense rule is: Never go out in the sun without protection from the sun's burning ultraviolet rays. A sunscreen or sunblock on exposed skin. A big, floppy-brimmed sunhat to further shield your face from the sun. And sunglasses to prevent squinting in the sun.

If wrinkles are gaining on you, make certain that

you're using only the mildest of soaps and the lightest of cleansing and face creams and lotions. Harsh soaps and strong astringents have no place on your dressing table. Select beauty masks with great care, and don't overdo their use. For special occasions, certain wash-off or peel-off masks can be helpful because they tighten the skin as they set. The effect is temporary but your skin will look smoother, smaller-pored, and less lined. That's because such masks stimulate the circulation; blood vessels in the inner layer of the skin expand and as they enlarge, fluid moves up to plump up the skin and make small lines less apparent. One homemade mask that has this smoothing-out effect is made from beaten egg whites. To use, first cleanse your face, then pat on a frothy, beaten egg white. Let it dry for a period of five to fifteen minutes. Wash off with tepid water. Nice for preparty use.

Fifty-Five Muscles to Mind

It's important to remember that you have no less than fifty-five facial muscles right under the surface of your skin. They're there to give expression and mobility to your face, not wrinkles. But if you constantly use some of them the wrong way, wrinkles are what you'll get. On the grimace checklist are such facial distortions as frowning, squinting, wincing, and glaring; and pursing, twitching, or biting the lips. How many of these do you do? And how often? If you need any convincing that the grimace habit is an age-tacker-on, do this. Next time you're sitting in a subway, bus, or train, study the faces around you. Which look the youngest? The ones with the relaxed, pleasant expressions, of course.

Hold Back the Line

In your continuing war against wrinkles, you know that you must handle your skin gently, no pulling and no stretching when applying or removing cosmetics. Here are some "finger exercises" to try, too.

For frown lines, practice "ironing" them away whenever you cream your face. With fairly firm strokes, work your fingers over the bridge of the nose up toward the hairline, then outward toward the temples. Repeat several times.

For those laugh lines around the nose and mouth, start at the chin, and using short, choppy strokes, work your fingers staccato fashion up the lines on either side toward the nose. Repeat several times. Also, puff out the cheeks fifteen or twenty times in quick succession.

For lines around the eyes, massage with a lubricating cream or oil, using your fingertips and a featherlight touch. Circle in under the eyes and out over the lids. Repeat, always starting from under the eye, working outward and up.

If eye crinkles are your big problem, don't forget to keep a little emollient or eye cream around the eye areas to protect against dryness whenever you're out in the sun or when you're sitting under a hair dryer or using a blow dryer. Very fine lines under the eyes can be helped by the application of a compress of warm facial oil. Lie down for ten minutes while you let oil-soaked pads rest on the eyes.

There are other antiwrinkle procedures. Cosmetic surgery, dermabrasion, skin peeling, and silicone injections are ways plastic surgeons and dermatologists combat the problem. And there are numerous antiwrinkle creams available at cosmetic counters. However, their effect is temporary. The tightening lasts only a few hours and the products tend to dry the skin.

Whatever else you do in your pursuit of a wrinkle-free face, avoid heavy makeup. It can turn the slightest line into a veritable crevice. Go easy on powder eye shadows that emphasize crepiness. Creamy is best. And when you apply foundation, blusher, and face powder, do so with a light touch wherever a wrinkle is lurking. And one final word of advice: Don't fret if you see a few wrinkles when you peer in your mirror. Worrying just makes them worse!

Liver Spots

They have nothing to do with the liver but that's the name these brown spots have been given for years. If you spend time in the sun without protection from those burning rays, you probably have a few liver spots on the backs of your hands, on your face, or on your neck. They really are like giant freckles but their color is darker and uneven and they don't fade away in the winter. Although they seem to occur as one ages, age is not the principal cause. Exposure to sun and wind over a long period is one reason behind their appearance. Hormonal changes play the major role in this condition. The production of melanin that gives the skin its color, is disturbed and the melanin that is produced clumps up in small, irregular, dark patches.

There are products especially formulated to bleach out these unattractive dark spots. Most contain hydroquinone or hydrogen peroxide. The process is apt to be slow and tedious; it takes a long time to bleach away the offending spots.

Dermatologists can treat liver spots much more quickly, and with better results, by freezing them for two or three seconds with liquid nitrogen or carbon dioxide, causing them to fade away. The process is called cryotherapy. Dermabrasion (skin planing with a high-speed brush or disc) and chemabrasion (a light skin peel using potent chemicals) are other ways of banishing the spots.

If your liver spots are not too prominent, you can easily camouflage them with a tiny amount of concealer matched to your own skin tone and topped with your usual tinted foundation.

A Scattering of Freckles

Poets celebrate them and movie stars flaunt them, but when the freckles are yours, you may feel less than joyous. Freckles are scattered melanin and you probably inherited the tendency toward them from your ancestors. Usually fair or red-haired persons who don't tan easily develop freckles. You can bleach them to make them less apparent—with lemon juice, peroxide, or one of the professional bleach creams, but the process is temporary at best and the treatment may dry or irritate your skin.

Disguise freckles, if you must, with foundation a shade darker than your skin but lighter than the freckles, followed with pressed powder or foundation in a shade close to your skin tone. And turn off future freckling by using sunblock preparations when you go sunning again.

Those Little Red Veins

Everything's going beautifully for you—no liver spots, no thinning hairline, hardly a wrinkle that shows, and then suddenly you see red in your magnifying mirror. Little red areas are visible on your cheeks, nose, forehead, or chin. Spidery little lines that go nowhere and seem to have no reason for existing. Alas, it's an annoying condition that often appears with age. In Europe it has a fancy name—*couperosé*. It almost sounds flattering but you know it isn't. In the United States, the identification is "broken capillaries." Or if you prefer, the official medical terminology—*telangiectasia*.

With aging, blood circulates through the capillaries nearest the skin surface very slowly and tends to stagnate. Those capillaries no longer are very elastic and the skin is so much thinner that the blood shows through. What to do? Avoid using too hot or cold water on your face; either one can aggravate the condition. So can too many spices and too much alcohol. Try not to face direct heat—no leaning into an open fire at a ski lodge or family room fireplace, for example. And try to avoid sudden temperature changes.

Since the skin overlying those small broken veins is extremely thin, it should be handled with great care and moisturized regularly. You might consider talking to a dermatologist about electrodessication in which an electric charge is used to close off certain veins to any further blood flow.

Late-Blooming Acne

The last time you worried about a pimple on your face was the day before the Senior Prom. And look at you now—twenty-five years later and suddenly you have a face full of teenage acne. Dermatologists say that they are seeing more adult acne now than ever. For some women, it's a resurgence of a skin problem they had when they were young. For others who survived their teens without an acne problem, the unexpected breakouts can be blamed on normal changes in the body's hormonal balance. Intermittent use of birth control pills is believed to be responsible for some cases of mature acne. Also, oil glands become unusually active during menopause for many women with acne eruptions the result. Other possible reasons, according to skin experts: increased air pollution, misuse of cosmetic products, and improper skin care.

Basically, acne is an inflammatory disease of the skin caused by overactivity and plugging of the sebaceous glands. It goes without saying that the skin must be kept meticulously clean, yet handled as little as possible. By all means, consult a dermatologist and follow his or her directions exactly. Left untreated, severe acne infections can cause scarred, pitted skin. This, in turn, requires more drastic treatment, such as dermabrasion, to level out scarred areas. Every case of acne differs so get advice for your own skin: don't copy someone else's treatment, hoping it will work for you. Your dermatologist probably will prescribe antibiotics, a hormone cream, benzoyl peroxide, or special lotions containing sulfur, resorcinol, or zinc oxide. He or she can set up a home program for you if you don't want to continue office treatments.

The Sun Is Your Undoing

"Every day you go out in the sun moves you further along in the aging process." That's the provocative word from Dr. Albert Kligman, professor of dermatology at the University of Pennsylvania Medical School. Dr. Kligman, who probably knows more about the human skin than Webster knew about words, says that what most women worry about are wrinkles, mottling, and a sagging, miserable-looking skin. And all of that is due to sunlight.

"There is an ugly way to age and there is a beautiful way," says the doctor. "The beautiful way is to stay out of the sun or protect yourself from its ultraviolet or burning rays."

Dr. Kligman asserts that the changes in skin that one normally associates with aging, are not due to age but to outside influences—sunlight, wind, rain, drying soaps, hard water, and harsh treatment—but basically sunlight.

"That means they are preventable," he declares. "Stay out of the sun or use a sunscreen and keep your youthful, unlined skin."

If there's anything worse that can happen to skin than sunburn, Dr. Kligman isn't sure what it is. Not only does the sun do damage to the skin's surface, but it damages the supporting structure—the collagen, elastin, and vascular tissues.

A SUNBURNED SKIN WILL NEVER HEAL. It may look normal but it's abnormal. The skin never recovers from a burn.

Every burn you get is a permanent inscription. The sunburn you get this year leaves that skin different than it was last year. It may not show immediately. In fact, there's a twenty-year difference between the time the damage occurs and when it becomes visible.

Which means the sunburn you got at that picnic on the beach when you were twenty is just showing up to help you celebrate your fortieth birthday.

Another fascinating fact from Dr. Kligman's sun-and-skin files: In people with equally sun-damaged skin, the person whose skin will look worse is the one more eloquent in terms of skin expressiveness. In other words, the one who "talks" with her face. The passive, nonverbal person will show less effect from the sun damage.

Sunscreens, Sunblocks, and SPFs

Does all this mean you have to abandon the idea of ever getting a warm, glowing tan, the kind that makes you look healthy, relaxed, and years younger? No indeed. Now it is possible to get a glorious suntan, safely, easily, and without fear of burning yourself to a crisp. Today's much-improved sunscreens and sunblocks let you safely increase the time you spend in the sun and give you just the protection your skin requires. Sunscreen ingredients like PABA (para-aminobenzoic acid), its derivatives, and benzophenones, absorb harmful ultraviolet light before it has a chance to get to your skin. And Sun Protective Factor (SPF) ratings tell you which product to choose. For example, if your unprotected skin usually burns in twenty minutes, a sunscreen with an SPF of 2 gives you protection from burning for about forty minutes. The higher the number, the more the protection.

If you're not already familiar with them, you should become acquainted with all the SPF ratings. The U.S. numerical rating system as approved by the Food and Drug Administration, is identical to one already in use in Europe so no need to worry. If you're travelling abroad, you can still identify your ideal sunscreen product.

Here are the ratings used to designate the relative effectiveness of and the limitations of sunscreens:

* SPF 2 to 4: minimal protection from sunburning; permits suntanning; recommended if you rarely burn and tan easily and deeply.

* SPF 4 to 6: moderate protection from sunburning; permits some suntanning; recommended if you tan well with minimal burning.

* SPF 6 to 8: extra protection from sunburning; permits limited suntanning; recommended if you burn moderately and tan gradually.

* SPF 8 to under 15: maximal protection from sunburning; permits little or no suntanning; recommended if you always burn easily and tan minimally.

* SPF 15 or greater: ultra protection from sunburn, offers the most protection; permits no suntanning; recommended if you burn easily and never tan.

Select sunscreens much as you would any cosmetic. Try different ones; then choose the product that not only promises protection, but that feels good on your skin. You wouldn't want to use an oily sunscreen, for example, on oily skin.

In general, sunscreens don't totally prevent tanning or burning. They just slow it down. And all sunscreens, even water-resistant types, should be reapplied liberally at least every hour, particularly after swimming and exercise, since water and perspiration reduce their effectiveness.

Tanning Rules

Sun protectors or not, the basic rules for tanning still hold: Start your suntan early in the morning or in the late afternoon. Stay out of the sun between 11:00 A.M. and 3:00 P.M. when the sun's rays are directly overhead and when ultraviolet radiation is at its peak.

And remember, wind, humidity, and high temperatures have a lot to do with the tan (or burn) you'll get.

Don't count on cloudy or hazy days being no-burn days. Clouds are made of water vapor and water transmits virtually all of the sun's radiation. Which explains why you can get burned while swimming in a pool, lake, or ocean. Sitting in the shade of an umbrella on a beach is no help either—the sand around you reflects those burning rays. They even penetrate thin cloth, especially when it's wet.

The sun hits hardest on cheekbones, tops of ears, and the nape of the neck. Other spots that need continuing attention are the eyelids, nose, lips, ears, tops of shoulders, backs of arms, backs of hands, backs of knees, ankles, and tops of feet. Body skin not usually exposed to the sun is supersensitive: You'll need a sunblock for your breasts and buttocks, an oilier sunscreen wherever skin is dry on the arms and legs. (Sunblocks are opaque and contain ingredients like zinc oxide that keep out both ultraviolet rays and light.)

Once you have a tan, you won't burn as quickly as you would otherwise. Nonetheless, a tan doesn't guarantee immunity; you should continue to use some protection, either a product with a lower SPF or a sunblock.

Many brands of lipstick, foundation, and other cosmetics now contain ultraviolet ray inhibitors. So do some hair products. All of which means you should be able to keep the sun a friend at all times, not an enemy. Or as Dr. Kligman would put it, you'll be able to "age the beautiful way."

4 / Happy with Your Hair?

QUESTION:

Guess what surveys have shown is the first thing other people notice about you and recall later? Answer: Your hair. (If you thought it was your eyes, you're almost right. Eyes rated in second place.)

So, with your hair permanently in the limelight—and you anxious to look younger and more attractive—it would seem to suggest that you'd better get a top-notch hairdresser. Or at least develop a certain skill with brush and comb.

Don't worry if you don't have the same gloriously thick shining mane you had ten years ago. Help is as close as your nearest hair care products aisle at the drugstore or supermarket or hairdressing salon. You can count on shampoos, conditioners, sprays, dandruff chasers, hair tamers, detanglers, and texturizers. And blow dryers, instant hairsetters, and curling irons. And rinses, tints, frostings, perms, straighteners, and much more. If you've got a hair problem, there's a cure for it. Even thinning hair or bald spots shouldn't make you lose sleep. There are natural-looking wigs and hairpieces to help you recapture that "crowning glory" feeling.

It goes without saying that in your stay-beautiful campaign, it's vital to take the best possible care of your hair. As you grow older, hair loses its elasticity and it also loses diameter. You must be gentle with it—less brushing and teasing and overdrying. Use a mild shampoo that adds moisture and then condition your hair to keep it from looking dry and dull.

A prime consideration should be how you wear your hair. A hairstyle that's all wrong for your features, an out-of-date style, can add years to your looks. The way you wear your hair should be compatible with the type of hair you have. It should flatter your features. And it should suit your life-style. A forty-year-old teller in pigtails could cause a run on a bank.

Do plan on making an appointment soon with a leading hairstylist in your area. You couldn't make a better investment. Get his or her advice about a youthful, flattering cut and style and accept the advice. Don't go back to your former teased-and-hair-sprayed bubble head in a week or two because you couldn't get used to soft, wavy, free-er or "looser" hair. You wouldn't want to be seen in public wearing a ten-year-old hat. Then why wear an out-of-date hairstyle? Everything else about you has changed or is changing—your wardrobe, your figure, your complexion, even your features. (It's the truth: As you grow older, your nose lengthens and your ears get larger. And eyes look smaller because of droopy lids and saggy muscles.) Admit it—it's time to try a brand-new hairstyle.

Incidentally, it's not true that hairdressers speak a language all their own, although many a woman, emerging from a beauty salon with a hairdo she dislikes, thinks so. The language problem usually pops up because one of the parties involved—namely, the client—says nothing.

The best way to talk to your hairdresser is just that—talk. Don't retreat into a private world of your own and sit silently through shampoo, tint, or set and come alive only to complain at the comb-out. Don't be cryptic when a hairdresser asks how you'd like your hair styled. "The usual way" is hardly specific enough.

And don't march in with a picture of a hairstyle torn from a newspaper or magazine and say, "I want this." The style that looks so captivating on the model may be completely wrong for your type of hair or face shape. If you do present a picture, make it a suggestion, not a command. Remember, you may have the hair, but your hairdresser has the experience and know-how. Tell him what you'd like; then listen. And if the final results please you, say so. Membership polls taken by the National Hairdressers and Cosmetologists Association indicate that the most frustrating thing that can happen to a hairdresser is to have a client depart without a comment, good or bad.

By the way, if you don't like a new haircut, don't fall apart. To be sure, hair grows fastest in women between ages sixteen and twenty-four—as much as seven inches a year. But even though it grows more slowly after middle age, it *does* grow. And very soon you'll be able to try another way of wearing it.

The Magic of Color

If you're short and yearn to be tall, you're pretty much out of luck. The same goes if you have blue eyes and wish they were brown. But if you're a brunet and long to be blond or a blond and want to be a redhead, you can do it.

Surveys show that no less than eighty percent of American women try changing the color of their hair at one time or another. Most opt for blond. For the mature woman it's a wise choice because, generally speaking, as you get older, lighter hair gives you a softer, more flattering look.

It's easy to make a hair color change; what isn't easy is deciding on the most becoming color. You must consider your skin tone. Even more important is the color of your hair at present. Be realistic. Don't think you can go from dark brown to ash blond in a twinkling. And before you do make this kind of radical change, be sure the new color is becoming. The quickest way to tell is to try on a wig although sometimes wig colors are not as animated as those from a hair-coloring product.

Also, to take color properly, your hair must be resilient and strong with no brittle or spongy ends. Your hairdresser may suggest waiting a few weeks until conditioning treatments restore it to health.

Streaking, frosting, tipping, or highlighting—those special procedures that give the effect of sunlight touching the hair—is an excellent way to initiate a color change. There are kits you can use to do the job yourself at home or let your hairdresser apply the sunshine. Once you see what lighter hair can do for your image, you may want to go on to a more dramatic change.

You should be familiar with all the color options available to you before you make a decision.

Rinses highlight natural color and tone down minor discoloration. Some can be used to tone lightened or tinted hair temporarily. They last from one shampoo to the next. Long-lasting rinses can darken, highlight, or restore original color and cover scattered gray hair. They gradually fade after about five or six shampoos.

Permanent tints make a definite change in hair color. They darken, lighten, or intensify your natural shade. Shampoo-in tints come in a variety of colors and are easy to use at home.

Then there's the two-color process which requires prelightening and toning. This is always necessary when hair color is being changed to a much lighter shade. Prelightening removes the natural color from the hair shaft; blond toner can then be applied.

All permanent hair coloring lasts until your hair grows out. When the new growth shows the original hair color, it's time for another treatment. Don't neglect to banish those dark roots as soon as possible. Why spoil the beautiful impact your new hair color has been making?

One advantage to streaking your hair is that you can wait up to four months or even longer to restreak —a comfortable margin if you're busy or traveling. Just how many streaks and where they should be placed depend on the color and length of your hair and how you wear it. A wise rule to follow is that the longer and darker your hair, the fewer the streaks.

Coloring hair does more than accent its beauty. It can also condition it, help control dryness, oiliness, split ends, and excessive limpness—something to remember if you have any of those pesky problems. And hair that has been colored usually has more body and holds a set longer.

When you look at a hair-coloring chart, remember that you won't get the exact shade the chart shows. The color of your own hair and the color of the product combine to give you an individual result.

Keep in mind that if you do make a dramatic change in the color of your hair, you may need to change your makeup to harmonize with it. You may even have to lighten or darken your brows with a brow pencil or crayon to avoid the possibility of an artificial look. At any age, "artificial" is bad, but for the mature woman, it's self-destructive.

A Word about Gray

You've heard the old saying, Pull out your first gray hair and wish on it—you'll get your wish. What you're much more likely to get is another gray hair replacing the one you removed.

Contrary to belief, gray hair is not dead hair. It's simply hair that has lost its natural pigment. No one is quite sure why hair loses its color. If it happens at an

A CHART TO HELP YOU CHOOSE
THE IDEAL HAIR COLOR

Skin Tones	Pale (Not predominately pink or golden)	Rosy (Pink to peach)	Olive (Ivory to golden)	Black (Tawny brown and mahogany)
Best Hair Colors	*Light honey blond *Strawberry blond and golden auburn *Light, medium or deep golden browns *Deep brunet (only if natural hair color is dark)	*Pale and ashy blond shades *Light ash brown and medium ash brown *Subtle, low-key auburns	*Dark golden blond *Light, medium, or dark golden browns *Dark, golden brunets	*Subtle auburns *Deep warm browns *Burgundy browns
Guidelines	Pale skin needs life—so a golden shade of hair color is best. Avoid anything too pale or ashy. Too dark is aging.	Minimize pink skin tones with low-key hair color in subtle ash shades. Avoid vivid blonds and fiery reds.	Brighten yellowish skin with vibrant hair color in warm golden shades of blond, brown, and brunet.	The deeper the skin tone, the darker and richer the hair color has to be. Stay away from ash shades. Avoid too light reds or golden shades.

Source: The hair color experts at Clairol.

early age, it is probably hereditary. Poor nutrition, a vitamin deficiency, poor circulation beneath the scalp, and even great stress or shock have been known to bring on gray hair.

Gray hair usually is looked upon as a badge of age. It tends to make women look older because often there isn't enough contrast between hair and skin. Gray hair and a youthful face can be a happy combination—many young women with gray hair wear it proudly but as a general rule, covering the gray will make you look younger. Of course if you have just a few scattered gray hairs, it's easier to live with them—they can look stylish, like frosting or streaking.

If you stay with your gray, avoid conservative hairstyles. Hair pulled back in a bun or braided can give you a definite grandmotherly look. Speak to your hairdresser about highlighting your gray hair just around the face—an ideal solution if your hair is only half gray, not totally so. Medium brown hair turning gray does well with a long-lasting blond rinse. And a long-lasting rinse in a gold-blond shade is a happy way to brighten up graying brown or blond hair. If you're a graying redhead, by all means try a pinkish blond rinse. And by the way, if you've been tinting your hair ever since you discovered your first gray hair, don't stop now. The shock could be enormous!

Get a New Look with a Perm

Perms are so versatile these days that practically every woman wants one. In fact, some fifty million women a year are either giving themselves home perms or getting them in salons. That's because today's perms can give you exactly the hair you want but don't have—curly, wavy, bouncy, and manageable.

The all-over frizzy perm, once almost a foregone conclusion when you had a perm, is strictly a matter of personal choice today. If you want tight curls, you can get them. But you can also use a perm to get softer curls and wider waves. And perms have really come into their own as a source of body for hair. With a body perm, your hair can go from flat to full and your hairstyle can gain more shape.

And now you can use a perm to redirect your natural curl into a more manageable pattern. For example, if you have extremely curly hair and want a smoother, yet still wavy look, a perm can reform your curl into a larger, looser one. Or, if the curl in certain areas grows in one direction and you would like to style it in another, you can perm just that section the way you want the curl to go.

Partial or spot perming is very popular now. Perm just the ends of your hair for curls at the nape of your neck. Perm just your bangs for a thicker, fluffier look. Or perm the crown hair close to the scalp to gain more height and fullness.

The new perms are quick and efficient to use. They're designed for every type of hair—fine, limp, bleached, and tinted. And home perms have never been better. They come with waving lotion, neutralizer, end papers, plastic turban, perm rods, and helpful instructions and styling suggestions. And not only do these home perms work faster, but they smell better, since the familiar ammonia smell has been eliminated in some home permanents. They use sulfite formulas rather than the long-standing thio formulas, thus doing away with that familiar "perm odor." Just as news-making are the perm kits designed to meet the special needs of color-treated hair. If you've heard that you can't perm your hair because you've had it frosted or used a shampoo-in tint, relax. There's a new, gentle, conditioning wave kit that will let you have just the curls, waves, or body you want and keep your hair color.

5 / Sorting Out Top Problems

Do you have a feeling that while the number of candles on your birthday cake is increasing, the number of hairs on your head is lessening? When you use a comb or brush are there enough hairs left on either one to build a bird's nest? Have you wondered lately why your forehead looks higher? Could be you have thinning hair. Some women go to the grave with more hair on their heads than Rapunzel had to let down over that balcony of hers. Others take to keeping their scalps covered up from an early age on—because, heavens know, their hair isn't doing the job.

Trichologists (hair health specialists) tell us that a single healthy scalp carries an average of 100,000 hairs, but there are wide variations in the count. Blonds have 140,000; brunets, 100,000. Redheads get the short count—only 90,000 hairs on their heads.

If you have a problem with thinning hair, the first thing to check up on is your general health. Poor health can affect hair noticeably, so schedule a physical examination with your doctor as soon as possible. Poor nutrition also affects the behavior of hair, so review what you've been eating to make sure that your diet is well-balanced and nutritious.

You could be abusing your hair without realizing it. Sharp bristles on hairbrushes, rollers that pull hair tight, and hairstyles that exert tension on the hair, all weaken it. So can strong chemical treatments such as hair straightening. To minimize hair loss, avoid the excessive manipulations of your hair. Shampoo it gently with lukewarm water and a mild shampoo. Blot it dry with a towel instead of rubbing it vigorously. Pamper it with conditioners and special scalp treatments; let it hang free and, whenever possible, let fresh air breeze through it. Thin hair should be permitted to relax on its own; it should never be pulled up and stretched back and pinned down. It's too fragile and breakable for that.

If you've got the time and the patience, make a rough count of the hairs that fall out and land on your comb or brush in the course of a day. It's perfectly normal to lose about 100 hairs a day, according to the experts. You may be worrying hairs off your head unnecessarily.

Fine Hair

In most cases, the word *baby* is pretty flattering until you line it up with fine hair. Baby fine hair may be soft and pretty to look at, but if you have it, you know what a problem it can be. It gets limp if you so much as pass by a steaming teakettle. It won't hold a curl or a set; it flies around, flattens down easily, is hard to manage, and it's prone to static electricity. So much for baby fine hair.

What can you do about it? Be gentle, very gentle. To promote more body and shine, brush it gently up from the scalp with a medium, natural bristle brush. Comb it gently with a wide-apart, round tooth comb. After shampooing, dry it with a hand dryer; then use the setting lotion you would for normal hair. (Those labeled for fine hair are usually heavier and thicker and can make your hair look lifeless.) Never use heavy conditioners and hair rinses nor shampoo with conditioning or balsam shampoos; they tend to make hair limp and soft, something you don't need. Avoid heavy hair sprays, friction, and tightly wound curlers. Indeed, any sort of friction or "pull" on your hair is verboten. Try a light body perm to put a little curl in your hair. Also, permanent hair coloring helps give fine hair a much fuller look.

Most women with fine hair hate to part with any of it but this is a big mistake. Leave it long and it gets stringy and lank-looking. Blunt-cut it the same length all around to give it bounce; its weight won't drag it down then. Remember, fine hair looks fuller when it's spanking clean. Don't skip any shampoo dates; you'll be sorry.

Oily Hair

Oily hair is demanding hair—it needs more attention, more shampooing, and more careful treatment than any other. Excessively oily hair becomes limp before you can put your comb away. The strands separate and refuse to hold a curl if you want one. Dirt from the air zooms in and settles on it. It encourages skin blemishes and soiled collars on clothing. In short, it's a real pain...but you can reduce the problem with constant vigilance.

Keep your scalp and hair scrupulously clean, shampooing every day if you must. Choose a detergent shampoo designed for oily hair and use warm water, not hot. Rinse thoroughly in clear water, then with warm water and lemon juice or vinegar. Finish off with a final clear water rinse. Between shampoos, freshen your hair by dabbing at the scalp with cotton dampened with alcohol and cologne. Or use a dry-powder shampoo.

Wash your comb and brush every time you wash your hair; otherwise you'll just be putting back oil in your hair. Covering your hairbrush with gauze will help blot up excess oil. And avoid brushing your hair vigorously—that merely spreads the oil at the roots of the hair faster through the hair. High heat stimulates oil production so turn your hair dryer to WARM and finish off with cool air. Avoid cream base conditioners; they'll only make your hair oilier and stickier than it already is.

Intricate hairdos are not for oily hair; wear your oily hair as simply as possible in a style that requires little or no setting. The less you manipulate your hair, the better. Try a short blunt cut to make frequent shampooing and drying less time-consuming. Blow dry styles are preferable. And by all means, try a light body wave. It will give your limp hair a much fuller look.

Curly Hair

Naturally curly hair is beautiful and always youthful. If you're trying to look younger and your hair is curly, you're already ahead. The newest perm techniques now make it almost impossible to tell a natural curl from an acquired one but both impart a marvelous look of bounce, fullness, and vitality to hair. But even something as delightful as curly hair can have problems. Naturally curly hair tends to frizz up with the least bit of humidity in the air. Often it's difficult to comb and set. Don't fight the curliness if you want to win the battle. Have a cut that complements it instead. Keep it short and make the most of a casual, tousled look. Or let it grow really long so that its own weight helps overcome the curl.

If you have curly hair, you know by now that bangs are out of the question. They refuse to be controlled. And don't plan on having your curly hair thinned; the short ends will just curl up and create an uneven bulkiness.

If you're striving for a sophisticated look rather

than a gamin one, talk to your hairdresser about relaxing the really tight curly sections of your hair—usually those around the hairline. After a shampoo, use a comb or blow dryer and brush to "stretch" your hair. In that way, you yourself can give it a temporary measure of straightening. Or try "wrapping," which works well with long hair. After a shampoo, wrap hair smoothly around and around your head, securing it in place with pins. Let it dry naturally. When you remove the pins and gently comb out your hair, you'll find that you have soft deep waves instead of the curl that all your friends envy.

Coarse Hair

Strong, heavy hair is categorized rather rudely in most hair manuals as coarse. Strong and wiry with lots of body, it is usually healthy, bushy hair and very hard to control. On the plus side, coarse hair takes well to color and perms. Cream rinses do much to soften and smooth it; hair sprays help control it after settings. Coarse hair becomes more manageable when cut and shaped by a professional, but there is much you can do to keep it at its best. Soften it with pomade and treat it to warm oil conditionings. Follow every shampoo with a cream rinse to give it more silkiness. Brush it often and thoroughly to get the natural oils right down to the ends of the hair. Reduce its bulk by tapering and layering—this technique works much better than thinning. If your coarse hair is also curly, you may want to settle it down a bit with a straightening treatment.

This type of hair is at its most manageable when it's kept short. Stay with simple hairstyles—elaborate ones just add to the possibility of your hair looking messy. When you set coarse hair, you should use large and jumbo-size rollers and make pin curls large and flat. Be sure to allow sufficient time for your hair to dry thoroughly. Don't rush to comb it out. If you do, it will merely snap back into its stubborn ways.

You might as well resign yourself to the fact that you're never going to be able to let your coarse hair out on its own. It needs you every moment. You've got to keep brushing and combing it, and don't work on the surface hair only. Get right down to the roots to loosen up and move those natural oils on out to the ends of the hair. Hair dressings are something you should explore—creams, lotions, and pomades can help make your independent hair behave. But stay away from heavy hair sprays; they'll emphasize that wiry look. Instead, use the soft, flexible type of spray for comb-through control. The bottom line, of course, is to cut and shape your coarse hair regularly.

Dull Hair

Dull, lifeless-looking hair is often hair that is simply coated with dust and grime from the environment. Stop using heavy conditioners, hair rinses, or shampoos with additives. These coat the hair, attracting dirt and dust. Don't fail to rinse out every last trace of shampoo when you wash your hair—rinse, rinse, and rinse again. Get out every last trace of shampoo and conditioner. Split ends nearly always add to an overall drab look; cut them off and keep your hair conditioned. Try highlighting drab hair—lightening selected strands of hair will give the whole head a shiny, burnished look.

Split Ends

There's only one answer to this problem: Cut them off. If you have split ends, you need a trim. Use a cream rinse after every shampoo. Don't use harsh lotions or hair spray that might make hairs stick together. Don't dry out your hair with overheated electric curlers or dryers. Other threats: too much sun and chlorine in pools. So, too, brush rollers and any undue stress on your hair. When your hair is wet rub on a dab of cream conditioner to give it more elasticity and to protect it during the setting and drying process. Wear it any length—but keep those split ends trimmed. That means a visit to your hairdresser at least every five to six weeks.

Dry, Brittle Hair

Dry, brittle hair tends to look lifeless and seldom smooth. Hard to curl, it's prone to static electricity and has an annoying flyaway quality. Tame it somewhat by using a cream conditioner as opposed to a liquid rinse. Step up scalp circulation with regular massaging or give your hair frequent, vigorous brushings. Use low or moderate heat settings on hair appliances and avoid heavy hair sprays or setting lotions. Don't stay out in the sun for long periods; if you go swimming, rinse out any salt or chlorine left in your hair. Chemical processes such as bleaches, permanents, and straightenings, can increase dryness and brittleness in hair. Two do-it-yourself treatments: Apply hair oil just to the dry ends; leave on for ten to fifteen minutes; then shampoo. Or rub a cream conditioner on your hair, wrap your head in a warm towel, and leave on for an hour before shampooing.

Whenever you have time after a shampoo, let your hair dry naturally, preferably outdoors in the sunshine and fresh air.

Dandruff

No one knows the exact cause of dandruff but it's not difficult to control with today's antidandruff products. Massage your scalp before a shampoo to loosen up the dandruff scales; then shampoo with an antidandruff product. Rinse and rerinse to wash away ever last bit of the shampoo from your hair and scalp. Don't ever scratch or dig at your scalp; you'll only irritate the condition. And don't aggravate it further by using a sharp bristled brush. A daily fingertip massage will help rev up circulation and keep your scalp "loose." Try to get plenty of sleep and relaxation. Emotional stress is said to have a lot to do with dandruff. If the condition becomes acute, see a hair specialist.

6 / The Magic of Makeup

By the time you've reached forty, your skin has changed, your hair color has changed, and your figure has changed—but what about your makeup?

Are you still using the same kinds of makeup and the same shades that you decided were right for you some years back? And applying them automatically— even hastily—in the same old way and in the same order? Some women make a ritual of the way they put on their makeup—and consider it bad luck if, for example, they start out by applying lipstick before mascara. Or blusher after lipstick instead of vice versa. Psychologists say that personal patterns like this help give a woman a sense of identity and security. As long as they don't get out of hand and dominate her to an extreme degree, such rituals are harmless.

One of the most rewarding and enjoyable things about cosmetics is their continuing variety. If you don't want to spend money on the full size of a new product, buy a small size or step up to a cosmetic counter and test the counter sampler. That's why they are there. Whatever you do, don't miss out on the fun of experimenting with new products, shades, and techniques. You may discover that the new lip pencil you bought in crushed berry red doesn't flatter your lips as much as your favorite precious plum lipstick. But the trial will not have been a total loss. After all, you did learn how to wield a lip pencil for the first time.

If you have doubts about your present makeup and the way you apply it; if you wish you could use makeup as skillfully as models do; if you wonder if there are ways in which makeup could make you look more sophisticated, younger, softer, healthier, even change the shape of your face as it were, there is an easy solution for you. Take a makeup lesson or lessons from an expert. Most major hair and/or skin care salons have resident experts ready to teach you the most effective way to apply your makeup. So that you won't forget what you learn, one thing they do is to apply makeup on one side of your face, then guide you while you, yourself, make up the other side, imitating exactly what they did. It's an excellent way to master professional makeup techniques.

Cosmeticians at cosmetics counters can be of great help, too. But since they usually have to take care of several customers at one time, you can't expect the same concentrated attention you will get from a scheduled lesson with a "makeup teacher." Also, keeping up with magazine, radio, and television beauty columns and programs, as well as with new beauty books, can help you update your skills with cosmetics. And if you're still putting lipstick on your upper lip, then biting your lips—or rubbing blusher or powder on your skin with the same energy you use to scrub a counter top, it's time for a change.

There are three preliminary requirements if you want your makeup to look perfect. Number one is good light. Number two is a suitable mirror. If it's daytime and at all possible, use natural light. You'll get a much truer picture of how the cosmetic shades you are using relate to your skin tones. If you are using artificial light, incandescent is preferable to fluorescent. Make sure the lighting is powerful enough and located where it illuminates your face evenly without distracting shadows. As for the mirror, have one large enough to reflect your entire face. Peering into a tiny, hand-held glass scarcely large enough to show one eye and a corner of your ear is not conducive to beautiful makeup. If your eyesight is less than perfect, work with a magnifying mirror by all means. There are excellent lighted mirrors available; some not only magnify, they also show how your makeup will look both in daylight and at night.

That third requirement? Organization. It will help enormously if you have all your cosmetics assembled in front of you. You shouldn't have to stop and rummage through a drawer to locate a lash curler or a cover-up stick. Keep everything you're going to need right at hand so that you can continue without interruption.

A Step-by-Step Makeup Lesson

There are many different ways of applying the various elements of makeup. Some experts recommend sponges or brushes. Some dote on makeup pencils. Others declare that there is nothing as good as your own fingertips. And not only do the experts differ regarding tools, but they have different sequences of makeup. One may dust the face with powder immediately after applying the foundation; another will wait until the last bit of blusher, eye-makeup, and lipstick are in place. Don't let any of these apparent conflicts disturb you. Makeup is highly personal, and makeup experts are entitled to develop their own favorite methods regarding its application. All of them have merit. What you have to do is read, study, and try for yourself. You may come up with a unique combination of tools and techniques that work perfectly for you. Stay with them—don't listen to your good friend who says you're wrong and she's right because *her* makeup expert came from Paris.

Here then, are some step-by-step instructions and assorted comments that will give you a sound grasp on making up "the way that models do."

1. Start with a totally clean face. Cleanse and moisturize your skin thoroughly before you so much as reach for a bit of makeup. The best way to apply your moisturizer is to dot it on your forehead, cheeks, and chin and then with long upward and outward strokes, using your fingertips or a sponge, draw it smoothly and evenly over your skin. It should cover every bit of your face. Do wait until it dries or "sets" before proceeding—you don't want your foundation to "run" or "slip."

   If you have very sallow skin, choose a tinted moisturizer to provide more clarity to your skin tone. And if you have an exceedingly oily complexion, you may prefer to use an astringent or freshener after cleansing and omit moisturizing.

2. Now is a good time to eliminate any circles or shadows under your eyes. Use a cover-up stick, a concealing cream, or a slightly lighter shade of your foundation and blend it under the eyes. Use it to camouflage those that extend from your nose to your mouth, too. Beware of using too light a shade; *never* use white. Concealer should always be applied stingily. Too thick and it will cake under your makeup. Pat it on, blend it lightly, and don't rub it in. That just moves it around; you want it to stay where the darkness is apparent. Blot lightly with a tissue to get rid of any excess oils. Repeat if necessary.

3. You're ready now for your foundation, that all-important "second skin" that can cover up so many flaws. Choose a liquid or cream formula if you have dry skin; a water-based or oil-retardant

one if you have an oily complexion. The shade should be as close as possible to your own skin tone. Put a large dab of foundation on your nose, chin, forehead, and cheeks. Because foundation contains color, you must work with it even more carefully than you did with your moisturizer. Again, using your fingertips or a sponge as you prefer, spread the foundation gently and evenly over your entire face, up to the hairline, down to the chinline. Don't leave a line of demarcation there—blend it well under the throat. Look carefully in the mirror at both sides of your face to be sure you have blended the foundation evenly there. Too many women look only at their direct head-on reflections in mirrors when making up—and never see the smudges and streaks on the sides of their faces.

4. Now dot on the blusher of your choice, cream or liquid. Cream lasts longer on certain skins— the kind that seems to absorb everything you put on it almost immediately. (As for powder blush—if you prefer that, hold off. You will want to apply it on top of a covering of face powder for more long-lasting effects.) Just where do you apply a blusher? Smile. See the "apple" of your cheeks? That's the spot. Put the blusher there; then blend it up and out back to the hairline. Never get your blusher too close to your nose; it draws the face inward and will make you look older. Keep it high and out toward the temples. So placed, you will find that it helps make your eyes look much brighter and more expressive. Also, a dab of blusher on the chin, in the center of the forehead, and close up to the temples and blended in thoroughly, will lend a healthy, vibrant look to your face. And if at first glance, you think you have put too much blusher on your cheeks, don't worry.

It looks prominent because you have no color yet on your eyes or lips. Once they are made up, the blusher's impact will lessen.

5. Now for the moment of high drama—your eye makeup. Before you begin, study your eyes so that you understand the "territory." There's the lid itself, extending from the lashes up to the crease. This crease or contour line marks the place where the lid indents. And above the crease is the browbone, a ridge that extends right up to the eyebrow. Basically, the rule for eye shadow is this: Choose three harmonizing shades of eye makeup: a shadow becoming to your eye color (and the clothes you plan to wear) and smooth that color over the eyelid. Look down into a mirror when you do this, stroking on the color, using a very light touch. Blend with your fingertip or a cotton swab. Color should go from lash line to crease of lid. Next, use an accent color in the eye crease to define the eye. Finally, apply a highlighter just below the eyebrow on the browbone, shading it down to the eye crease.

Another good rule to remember: Use discreet colors during the day; brighter hues at night. You want your eye makeup to enhance your eyes, not drown them. Your choice of color also depends on the shape of your eyes. Puff lids look better with dark colors; use nothing light or glittery on them to stress that fleshy look. Deep-set eyes come forward when you put a pale shade above the lashes, and blend a darker shade above the crease and under the browbone. If you have a heavy lid, use a dark shade on the lower lid, light eye shadow below the bone.

If you have certain unattractive eye conditions—lots of creases and wrinkles in the area, an overhanging browline, or puffiness, you may be better off playing down your eye makeup. One expert says that the best thing a mature woman can do to bring back clarity and focus to the eye is to eliminate eye shadow and use just a pencil liner. Line the *inside* upper and lower rims with dark pencil. (It will take practice— it's tricky.) Smudge a little of the same dark pencil over the lash line. That, plus mascara, and you will have beautiful eyes without calling attention to any flaws.

Many cosmetic companies make life easier for us all by offering eye shadow compacts containing duos or trios of harmonizing colors so that we don't have to spend the entire day at a cosmetics counter trying to pick flattering shades. For blue eyes, some experts recommend plum, charcoal, gray, brown, muted green, and muted turquoise as wise choices. For green eyes, consider plum, brown, muted blue, navy blue, or muted turquoise. For hazel eyes, try muted green, muted blue, muted turquoise, plum, brown, or yellow-gold. Brown eyes can wear just about any color as long as it's not too bright.

You'll be faced with choices, too, in the type of eye makeup you select. Creams and powders are easiest to use, although some women find that cream shadows tend to slip; others avoid powder shadows, especially the frosted ones because they accentuate crepiness. Pencils are easy to use and convenient to carry. When you use them, be extra careful—don't use them with such force that you pull at the delicate eye-area skin. Eye shadows that you brush on mixed with water have good points: They stay on longer, can be reduced in color intensity when thinned with water, and don't collect in the eye creases.

6. To use an eyeliner or not—that is the question.

And the answer is up to you. Brush it on or apply it with a pencil—whatever you do, don't circle your eyes with a raccoon-look. Any well-defined line will look harsh and outdated. Apply the liner just above the upper lashes, smudging it so that it looks blurred. Widen the line slightly at the outer edges of the eye to give a "lift" to your expression.

7. Mascara is probably the single most beautifying cosmetic you use; never ignore it and take plenty of time to apply it properly. If you perpetually complain that your mascara beads and sticks to your lashes so that they clump up into little spikes, it's most likely because you're applying mascara to lashes that are not perfectly clean. Make certain your lashes are clean and separated before you start. Bend the upper lashes gently upward between your thumb and forefinger or use an eyelash curler on them. Always use one hand to hold the mascara brush or wand; the middle finger of the other hand to gently lift the outer corner of your eye upward. This lets you get the wand closer to the roots of the lashes. Apply mascara first on the top of the upper lashes from the inner corner of the eye out. Then raise brows with the fingertip to do the underside of the lashes. Do the bottom lashes next. Let the mascara dry completely; then apply a second coat. Be sure each lash is separated from its neighbors—you can do this by brushing them with a clean lash brush or lash comb once the mascara is dry.

Basically, mascara comes in cake and in cream forms. Cake mascara must be dampened with water, then applied with a brush. It takes more time than other forms but lets you obtain just the consistency you want. It's especially good for thin, fragile lashes. Cream mascara squeezed from a tube onto a dry brush lets you build up the mascara on your lashes a little more thickly. Automatic mascara wands are the easiest of all to use—one wand even lets you dial just the amount of mascara you want for light, medium, or heavy applications. And there are special thickening and lengthening mascaras and waterproof ones that let you cry, swim, or splash water on your face and still retain your "fringes." Black or black-brown mascara is the best choice for brunets; soft brown or charcoal for blonds and redheads. One final tip: Use eye makeup removers to take off your mascara; don't depend on cleansing cream or soap to do the job.

If your eyelashes are so pale that they're practically invisible, think about having them dyed. It's best to have the job done by a professional. The dye used is vegetable-based and the process takes about fifteen minutes. Your lashes will stay dark as long as four weeks.

8. Don't overlook your eyebrows—they're an important asset, framing and setting off your eyes. Keep them well groomed but don't pluck them just before you start putting on your makeup. You'll have to cope with a reddened brow if you do. Instead, brush them up and out into a smooth line. If they're sparse and need a little color for thickness, fill them in with a few light strokes of a brown eyebrow pencil. *Never* trace the shape of your brows with a definite penciled line; it's not only a dated technique (shades of Jean Harlow), but it can be extremely aging.

9. When you get to the point where it's time to apply your lipstick, you're almost finished with your lesson. For the most professional look of all, first outline your lips with a lip brush or

pencil, in a shade slightly darker than the lip color you plan on using. That outline helps give the best possible shape to your lips and prevents your creamier lip color from edging up into any annoying vertical lip lines you may have. Once the outline is completed, fill in your lips with your lip color. Then dust a little powder over your mouth and reapply the lip color for a long-lasting effect. Choose a lip color that coordinates with your blusher and with the clothes you are wearing. A soft, romantic shade is a better choice for the mature face than a brilliant red one. Bright reds can be harsh and overpowering; you're more apt to get a cheery, young look when you stay with a warm, rosy color.

10. If you like a soft, matte look for your makeup, now's the time to dust your face lightly with translucent powder. A face that is crisscrossed with little lines and creases, however, may not take kindly to a powdery dusting; powder tends to settle in wrinkles. If you have a very oily T-zone—nose, chin, and forehead—try powdering that area only to keep down the shine.

Are You Making the Most of Fragrances?

History tells us that fragrances have always been important cosmetics for women. Egyptian women in the days of the pharaohs used to annoint their bodies with sweet-smelling ointments; in early Rome, well-bred women bathed in perfume. So did their Greek counterparts. But somehow, even though baths went out of fashion by the Middle Ages, women didn't abandon perfume. They used it to cover up less pleasant odors. During the time of Louis XIV, the seventeenth-century French "Sun King," washing clothes and personal hygiene were not regarded as important. Instead, they were replaced by the lavish use of perfumes. If nothing else, the Royal Court gatherings must have been odoriferous.

Fragrances have lived through other colorful eras. Not so long ago in this country, it was mainly regarded as something to be worn by the privileged few. Good perfume was expensive. It was something to be acquired—and used—on special occasions only. You received a bottle of perfume, toilet water, or cologne for a birthday or Christmas, then put it on display on a dresser top, only using it for important social events. Eventually, it evaporated or discolored because it was left in the sun or heat.

It's a different scene today. Dresser tops are crowded with perfumes and other types of scents including spray colognes, bath oils, perfumed body lotions, solid perfumes, and sachets. And they don't get a chance to evaporate or fade away. They're being used lavishly and constantly.

People who are involved in perfume sales say that young people are the ones who are responsible for the explosion in fragrance sales. They are adventurous about perfume; they have definite opinions about what they like; and they don't follow the old idea about adopting a "signature scent."

There's nothing wrong with a "signature scent"—if you happen to like one particular fragrance and wear it constantly so that people identify you with it, good for you. What you've done is create a fragrance aura that is very much your own. But a word of caution: Sometimes, particularly as one gets older, it is very easy to get into a rut. With bright red lipstick, for example. Or blue eye shadow. Or a fragrance that is heady with attar of roses. Why not be flexible and experiment with other cosmetics, other fragrances?

Different fragrances hold different messages. They are sporty, alluring, romantic, sexy, elegant, and outdoorsy. And they not only give that message to you, the wearer, but to everyone around you. So your challenge is to select a perfume with the right message for the occasion. Don't wear a sexy, sensual perfume to the supermarket, for example.

It's not difficult to know what a perfume is saying when you understand the qualities implicit in the seven basic types of fragrances. Florals, either single or floral bouquets, are usually endearing and nostalgic. Spicy perfumes are briskly pungent; woodsy-mossy scents are warm and refreshingly forestlike. Exotic Orientals are heady, while the fruity perfumes can be crisply citrus or mellow like peach or apricot. Then there are the modern blends that hint of sophistication in their bright sparkle.

Whatever you do, don't select a perfume because it's all the rage or because your closest friend adores it. You won't ever be sure that it's your own—and that's what perfume should mean to you—something that says you. It should never be a copycat affair.

Read up on perfume advertising. Some of the best copywriters in the business create those exact definitions to tell you what mood a certain fragrance can create. Go to a perfume counter and try out the testers there. But not too many different scents at one time, please. Three is about all your inexperienced nose can separate and evaluate. Buy sample sizes and the less expensive forms of a fragrance until you find one that appeals to you.

And don't overlook "layering"—using many forms of the same scent to establish a fragrance mood. Start out in the tub with perfumed soap, bath oil, or other bath additives. Step out and continue with a cologne spray, toilet water, perfumed body moisturizer, and/or dusting powder. When dressing, apply your perfume. Where? In all the usual places and then some. The long-touted pulse points still are good: at your temples, the base of your throat, on your inner arms at the elbow, the wrists, over the heart, and at the back of the knees—wherever body temperature is slightly higher.

Remember, you should reapply perfume at least every four hours. It's not forever, especially in overheated, crowded rooms or outdoors in strong sunlight or in cold or wet weather.

You should never dab on toilet water or cologne—dabbing is strictly a perfume technique. Toilet water and cologne are meant to be used lavishly. If they are not already in a spray form, use them in an atomizer so that you can diffuse them more effectively.

There are clever new ways of using fragrances for you to explore. Fragrance pencils are one example—slender little wands of perfume in a waxen base. Then there are touch-tip concentrates—colognes in slim bottles with sponge tops to press to your skin and thus scent it.

And also look into the new "environmental fragrances"—such as perfumed candles, potpourris, pomanders, perfume drawer liners, incense, and more. They can literally surround you right at home with their scented messages.

Finally, whenever you choose or wear a fragrance, remember that it should please you first of all—make you feel more confidently beautiful and self-assured. If you're not emotionally aware of your fragrance, it could be the wrong one for you. A fragrance is intended to be the subtle, finishing touch to your total makeup. It should be personal, it should be enjoyable, and it should be memorable.

7 / The Beauty Bath and More

According to history, Elizabeth of Hungary was so beautiful at the age of seventy that she bestirred a burning passion in a young man of twenty-six. And to what did she attribute her enduring appeal? Her beauty bath. It seems that she dunked her septuagenarian self regularly in a tub filled to the brim with warm water containing among other things, lemon and orange peel, dried mint leaves, and her favorite perfume. We make no promises about passionate young men but we do suggest that a luxurious, indulgent bath will go a long way toward erasing those tension lines, fatigue grooves, and worry furrows from your face. Furthermore, it will brighten, smooth, and soften your skin and refresh, revitalize, and relax you. That should be reward enough.

You can take a bath just to get clean. Or you can turn it into a genuine beauty adventure. Bath and body products have never been as numerous. Among them are bath oils, bath salts or crystals, bubble baths, bath gels, milk baths, bath foam concentrates, even bath "pearls." Toss a handful into the water and they dissolve into fragrant oil.

And then there are the soaps—all sizes, shapes, colors, and fragrances. By the bar or by the bottle. You can lather up with a soap that scents the bathwater with the aroma of roses or use a cooling, natural sea moss gel that reminds you of a remote ocean bay. And the bath tools. Like a long-handled back brush or a bath mitt, a big, squashable sponge or a loofah, that rough-textured vegetable gourd perfect for rubbing away dead skin and leaving the body atingle. And don't overlook a bath pillow to let you lie back and completely relax. A bathtub tray to let you have everything right at hand for an in-tub manicure. And a bath thermometer to assure you that you're stepping into just the right temperature water.

And the pampering needn't end when you get out of the tub. A galaxy of afterbath products can help you soften, polish, and perfume your skin. Bath perfumes and colognes, afterbath splashes and friction lotions, spray talcums, dusting powders, body moisturizers, lotions and more, are available. Growing in popularity are the "body regimen" products—creams, gels, and special massagers with which you can tone up hips, thighs, buttocks, and upper arms. Bathtime is ideal for their use.

The Rules of the Bath

Everything in life has rules, including taking a bath. You must start with an absolutely shiny, clean tub. If a cleanser has been used to get rid of a bathtub ring, make sure that every bit of it is washed away. Use a bath thermometer to check the water temperature. These are the Fahrenheit degrees at which hydrotherapists distinguish baths, by the way: cold (less than 65°F); cool (65°–75°); neutral or tepid (75°–85°); warm (85°–100°); and hot (over 100°). Cold for a stimulating in-and-out plunge with quick soaping and rinsing. Cool for a quick pickup after a long day at work. Neutral or tepid for a cooling, refreshing break when the weather is hot. Warm for your "escape bath"—the one when you stretch out and relax for as much as twenty minutes. (Use your common sense, though, about how long you linger in your tub—if you have very dry skin, oversoaking is not for you.) Hot—for easing stiff muscles but not a bath to linger in. Very hot water can be deenergizing and drying to the skin.

What to put in your beauty bath? You'll find that bath oils are a wise choice especially if you have very dry skin. They leave an invisible, softening film on your skin. Bath gels also have special skin-soothing properties. Bath salts and crystals could be drying if your skin is supersensitive but they're ideal for the bather who wants a water-softening, fragrant additive. If you like the look and feel of a bath piled high with foamy bubbles, add your bubble bath while the water is running into the tub. Enjoy them for a while before you start lathering up; soap can reduce the bubbles quickly.

Give special consideration to the soap you choose as a tubmate. Don't pick a soap because its color matches that of your shower curtain. Dry skin, for example, relates well to superfatted soaps. Oily skin gets along with glycerin soaps which soften and smooth but are nonfatty. Medicated soaps help skin aggravated by blemishes. "Soapless" soaps lather generously in hard water because of their detergent and emollient ingredients. They're nonalkaline and many contain face creams or other emollients that leave a pleasant effect.

Stretch Out and Wiggle

Use cleansing cream on your face before you get into the tub, and pat a little eye cream around the eye areas. Or apply your favorite mask. Dip cotton squares in witch hazel and place them over your eyes after you're in the tub and leaning blissfully back on your bath pillow or on a folded towel. Relax completely for ten minutes or more. Stretch out. Let your body float. Wiggle your toes. Relaxing like this before you start soaping eases tired muscles, loosens perspiration and soil, and makes your pores more receptive to cleansing. If the water in the tub cools while you're soaking, add a little hot water.

When you feel you have relaxed enough, get on with your cleansing. Soap your body thoroughly and use a bath brush or friction mitt to stir up circulation and slough off dead skin. Give special attention to your upper arms, elbows, shoulders, knees, and feet.

If you have a bath tray on which you've placed manicure items, a tweezer, pumice stone, and mirror, now's a good time to put them to use. Whatever you do, don't step out of the tub with soapsuds clinging to you. It's important to rinse away every last bit of soap or you're encouraging dry skin. Use a spray attachment for rinsing off, or if you don't have one, let the warm water out of the tub and replace it with clean, cooler water and splash about in it briefly.

Once completely rinsed, you're ready for toweling. Pat yourself dry and then with gentle but firm strokes, rub a moisturizing body lotion or cream over your entire body. Or, if you prefer, envelop yourself in fragrant bath powder. Or spray cologne. The choice is yours. Slip into your robe and give yourself a manicure or pedicure or both. Or you may want to do some defuzzing.

The point is: Make the most of this private relaxing time; do whatever it is that you tend to postpone doing to keep yourself in perfect condition. Once you develop the habit of pampering yourself in the bath, you'll notice a definite improvement in your total appearance. Spending a quiet time like this can make you more keenly aware of all the things you could be doing to improve your skin, your hair, and your nails. And you'll start doing them.

And If You Prefer Showers

Just because you prefer showers doesn't mean you have to miss out on the luxury touches tub bathing affords. Most fragrant soaps, gels, and oils are packaged for shower devotees. Some come in unbreakable tubes, often with cords or hangers attached so that you can hook them conveniently over the faucet or on your wrist. Mixed with water, these cleansers foam up and can be worked into the skin with a mitt, washcloth, or brush. Or you can smooth on a bath oil all over your body before turning on the water and get the same skin-soothing, cleansing benefits under the shower that you would in a tub.

In a tub you can always slide down and soak your back in the soapy water. It's a different story in a shower: You've got to have a back brush and soap to reach between your shoulder blades.

By varying water temperatures you can turn your shower into a fatigue-relieving experience. Alternating with hot and cold water, turn the water spray against your body. Switch from hot to cold and back to hot three or more times. Don't forget to let the water play against your feet and legs as well as against your torso. Dry down with a fairly vigorous toweling and use an afterbath lotion or friction rub. You'll feel completely refreshed.

Whether it's a tub or shower, don't fail to set aside an extra-long, leisurely time once or twice a week for your beauty spa experience. Very soon you'll agree with the ancient proverb: Water is the most healing of all remedies, and the best of all cosmetics.

Water, Water Everywhere

To make the most of water as a beauty aid, you must do more than soak in it. It must be taken often and properly, inside as well as out.

A healthy person can survive for weeks without food but only a week or less without water. The average adult body contains about forty-five quarts of water and loses about three and one-half quarts a day. The recommended intake of water for most people is six to eight glasses a day, using an eight-ounce glass. Liquids such as coffee, tea, and milk that contain water, don't count as part of the daily requirement because of their other ingredients—caffeine, tannic acid, and fat.

Time for a Change

Many women have the mistaken notion that as they grow older, they no longer need to worry about body odor or excess body hair. It is true that sweat glands decrease in size due to hormonal changes. You may not perspire as much as you did when you were a self-conscious teenager at your first dance. But your skin still has some three million sweat glands, all quite capable of exuding perspiration. And as far as body hair goes, for some women the growth of superfluous hair on their arms, legs, and underarms does slow down. For others, it can tend to become more profuse.

But for most mature women, the truly startling change as far as excess hair goes, is the sudden appearance of coarse facial hair where there was none before. "Wild" hairs appear and ruin the smooth line of one's eyebrows. Hair growth becomes more apparent on the upper lip and single "whiskers" pop out around the chin area. Most of these hairs are gray, possibly because a sun-induced enzyme decrease halts the pigment-making process. All of them are a definite nuisance. If your eyesight isn't good or if you don't have a strong magnifying mirror, you may be missing yours. Better check.

Wetness and Odor Control

At any age, underarm odor is usually the major offender in the body odor department. Its main cause is the action of skin bacteria on secretions of the apocrine sweat glands abundant in the underarm area. Rule one in controlling this odor is absolute cleanliness. Removing underarm hair helps reduce the number of bacteria present. If you perspire very little, washing with soap and water and using a deodorant may be all you need. Deodorants are designed to counteract perspiration odor whereas antiperspirants inhibit perspiration flow and control odor.

The best time to apply either one is at night, just before going to bed when sweat glands are the least active. Don't apply either one right after shaving the underarm area; your skin is sensitive then and easily irritated. If you've just bathed or showered, be sure your skin is well rinsed; any soap left on the skin can interfere with the action of a deodorant or antiperspirant. And wait until the skin is thoroughly dry before applying.

Something to watch out for is perspiration odor trapped in clothing, particularly sweaters, jackets, woolens, and any heavy winter wear. Put on fresh clothing daily; wash or dry-clean clothing that has acquired an odor and get rid of any garments (usually synthetics or poorly dyed fabrics) that seem to encourage perspiration and odor.

When Hair Is Superfluous

It's ironic that just when you want the hair on your head to stay put and thicken in, it starts thinning, but the fuzz on your face, arms, and legs often becomes more apparent. In most instances, it may be best for you to continue using the same methods of removing excess body hair that you've been using right along. If you have a very light growth of hair on your arms and legs, you may be better off leaving it alone. If the growth is dark, you might bleach it to make it less noticeable.

Shaving is the quickest, easiest, and least expensive way to remove unwanted hair. Use a safety or electric razor and try to avoid scraping or nicking the skin. Hair that is water-softened is easier to shave, so make shaving part of your bathtime routine. Shave your legs upward in long, even strokes. Don't shave your forearms, face, or sensitive body areas. It's not true that shaving makes hair grow back thicker. Shaving removes hair at the skin's surface and the hairs are blunt-cut so they feel more bristly. Also, when the hair is dark, early regrowth or a stubble is quickly visible.

Regrowth is not quite as apparent when you use a depilatory. Depilatories dissolve the hair somewhat below the skin's surface. Results last about a week. Be sure to follow the directions very carefully, not only about how long to leave the product on your skin, but also regarding the time interval before you can safely reapply it. The best time to use a depilatory is just before taking a shower—then you can easily wash away both the preparation and the dissolved hair.

Waxing works for four to six weeks but it's much trickier than shaving or using a depilatory. A thin layer of melted wax is applied to the skin, allowed to cool, then stripped off, pulling the hairs from just below the surface of the skin. You can do it yourself with a home-waxing kit or have it done in a salon. Waxing can be more comfortable when done by a professional.

And then there's electrolysis—the permanent way to remove superfluous hair. It can be expensive and time-consuming but it does the job for keeps. A fine needle is inserted down to the root of the hair, an electric current is sent through for a fraction of a second, and then the dead hair is plucked out with tweezers. There are home electrolysis kits on the market but they call for more proficiency and skill than you may have. If yours is a problem growth of hair, ask your doctor to recommend a professional electrologist.

Specifically, Facial Hair

Depending on how conspicuous it is, how heavy, how dark, and on what part of the face it grows, you can either camouflage or remove your unwanted facial hair.

If the hair is relatively fine, bleach it with a commercial bleach or with one you concoct yourself. Mix thirty-percent peroxide with a little ammonia and water. Swab on where needed; it may take two bleachings done twenty-four hours apart to strip the hair completely of color. One bleaching may just accentuate a yellowish or reddish hue, making the hair more apparent than ever. Rinse off the bleach thoroughly and apply a little emollient cream to the treated area.

Tweezing is an easy practical way to get rid of isolated hairs on the face and for shaping eyebrows. Swab the area first with an astringent-soaked cotton pad. You'll probably have to repluck after two or three weeks. Never pluck a hair growing from a mole or wart. Check with a dermatologist first.

For a heavier growth of hair on the upper lip, cheeks, or chin, use a depilatory specifically marked "for facial use." Follow the directions carefully; keep it well away from your eyes and do not apply an astringent or use soap on the treated areas immediately afterward.

A salon waxing may be your happiest solution to the problem of facial hair. However, since waxing removes both fine and coarse hair, you'll discover that face powder won't cling to your skin as well as it did previously.

Whatever method of hair removal you choose, the length of time between treatments depends on the rate of growth of your hair. Depilatories should not be used more often than every two weeks; waxing demands a four- to six-week delay—you have to wait until the hair grows out enough for the wax to get a good "bite" on it. A razor can be used as frequently as you like; likewise, a tweezer. You're the best judge of when it's time for defuzzing again.

8 / Help for Your Hands and Feet

Did you ever go to a palmist and wonder how in the world she could know so much that was personal about you? Your hands told her. Their shape and appearance, the condition of the skin, the way your fingernails looked, and even your handclasp provided her with clues.

Ask yourself if on any given day you'd want a palmist—or anyone, for that matter—to study your hands. Do you keep them perfectly groomed at all times so that they can be on show? Or do they usually look so grubby and untended that you bury them in your pockets or tuck them behind you out of sight? And what does your handshake say about you? (If it's firm but gentle and your skin feels soft and smooth, you've left a young impression.)

True, it's a fact that hands are quick to betray age. The skin on the back of the hand is soft and fine, with sebaceous glands and sweat gland openings. But the palm is coarser. It has sweat glands but unlike most other parts of the body, no sebaceous glands. This means that it is one of the dryest parts of the body. Hand skin endures hard use and tends to thin out with age. Veins show through it dramatically. Neglect hand care and the problems are emphasized. Take good care of them and you minimize the flaws.

Start off by protecting your hands from weather extremes—too much sun, cold, temperature, harsh wind, and rain. And protect them, too, from daily wear and tear. Whenever you wash your hands, use lukewarm water and plenty of soapsuds to get rid of grime and dead skin cells. Massage in those soapsuds, going up beyond the wrists. Rinse well—again in lukewarm, never cold, water—dry thoroughly and rub in a hand cream or lotion. Be generous with it and wring your hands à la Lady Macbeth so that every bit of skin gets some of that vital moisturizing.

Gloves Are Good Friends

Make gloves a part of your from-now-on-beautiful-hands campaign. It may sound overwrought to you but if your hands are red, rough, and in really bad shape, pile hand cream or petroleum jelly on them lavishly, pull on a pair of cotton gloves, and go to bed. In the morning you'll find your hands feeling and looking much better. Get yourself a glove wardrobe: cotton-lined, waterproof gloves for household tasks involving water. Heavy fabric gloves for gardening or heavy chores. Cotton gloves for dusting and other light tasks. But don't keep on those waterproof gloves, even cotton-lined, for an extended period of time. The moisture and perspiration that can accumulate when you wear them too long can irritate the skin. You know, of course, that in cold weather you should wear gloves or mittens for all outdoor expeditions. Not to do so is to guarantee yourself two very red, rough, chapped hands—and that's not beautiful!

Why Changes Occur

If your nails give you more trouble in the winter, there's a reason. Nails go into hibernation in freezing weather and grow at only half their normal rate (about one tenth of an inch monthly). Ordinarily it takes a fingernail about four months to grow from its base to cutting length. Nails grow faster in the summer and faster on the right hand than the left. You won't be as intrigued with this news—nail growth slows down as you age and nails develop ridges and split more readily.

The natural oils that keep nails flexible tend to dry out in cold weather, leaving them brittle and more susceptible to breakage. But it's not all weather. The use of strong detergents can weaken nails. Pushing back the cuticles with a metal instrument can cause white spots on nails. Cutting cuticles, instead of gently pushing them back, increases the probability of hangnails. And vitamin deficiencies or illness can result in discoloration, splitting, and ridging.

Once the inherent hardness of nails depended on heredity, diet, and environment. Now it's how quickly you can get to your manicurist. Even if you have thin nails that break, split, or peel easily, you can bolster them with protective coatings, many reinforced with acrylics and nylon. There are waterproof, detergent-resistant mending tissues to salvage broken nails. And glue-on fake nails to tide you over. Or even sculptured nails that are like extensions of your own. A thick liquid is used to built them up. When the liquid hardens, it can be shaped with an emery board. About every two weeks, as the nails grow out, a fill-in liquid is applied to smooth the surface.

All about Manicures

If you are able to have a professional salon manicure every week, that's good news for your nails. But there's no reason why you can't give yourself the same kind of manicure at home. Start by removing the old polish. Then, with an emery board, file the nails into oval shapes, working in one direction at a time from side to center. Nails are layered like an onion, so don't seesaw back and forth with your file or they'll start peeling. Don't file too low at the corners; let each nail extend a little over the flesh to give it a good firm base. For problem nails, square off the tops to help make them stronger. Next, massage a lubricating cream around the base of the nail and the surrounding finger area to stimulate circulation and soften the cuticle. Thereafter, soak your fingers in warm soapy water for five minutes or so; if necessary, scrub gently with a natural bristle nailbrush to remove grime. Dry each nail gently with a towel and apply cuticle remover around the base of each one.

With an orangewood stick wrapped in cotton wool and kept moist by dipping in soapy water, push back and lift the cuticle gently away from the nail. Clip any loose pieces of cuticle only; don't cut into cuticles recklessly; you'll create hangnails. If you notice any stains along the sides of the nails, remove them with a cotton-wrapped orangewood stick dipped in peroxide.

Now massage a little hand lotion into your hands and on your fingers; wipe your nails free of all traces of moisture or cream and prepare to apply polish. If your nails aren't particularly healthy, this is a good time to rev up circulation and strengthen them by buffing. Using a nail buffer, buff in one direction for only about one minute per nail. Longer, and you risk getting the nails overheated.

Which hand should you put the polish on first? If

you're right-handed, start with the right hand. You'll be more adroit and find it easier to apply polish on your less efficient hand without smearing. And should you work from your little finger to your thumb or vice versa? Some say it's easier to work from the outside in. Others point out that the thumbnail is broader, takes more polish, and needs more time to dry. We say take your pick; just get the polish on smoothly.

Using a sweeping central stroke from the nail base to the tip, then one stroke on either side of that first one, and apply a base coat. This prevents the nail color pigment from discoloring your nails. Make it two coats of base, if you like. Then two coats of nail enamel. Plus a top coat or sealer to help protect the nails and prevent chipping. Finish up by running an orangewood stick tipped with cotton and dampened with polish remover along the edge of the cuticle and fingertips to remove any smudges of polish. And remember, two coats of base, two coats of enamel, and one coat of sealer add up to five. It's going to take time for those five layers to dry, so don't rush out and start unraveling stitches in the sweater you're knitting or planting an herb garden. Let the polish harden completely. Otherwise, expect smears and smudges.

Hands and Fingertips

Stains on your fingers? Use lemon juice or peroxide to remove them. Moisturize your skin well after each application because either one is drying.

Discolored areas on the backs of your hands? Bleach out with bleach cream (it takes time) or conceal with waterproof cover-up cream. Use it to help conceal veins as well. If brown spots are very noticeable, check with a dermatologist.

Swollen veins? Models learn to keep their arms crossed in front of the body, waist high, with their hands and palms turned upward. It's a graceful pose and youthful. Practice it when you can. Keeping your hands elevated whenever possible helps their appearance because it minimizes swollen veins.

White knuckle look? Don't grip your hands together tightly; join them in a light clasp.

Hands too large or too small? Be selective about jewelry. Enormous rings and collections of heavy bracelets on small hands or on very heavy hands simply focuses attention on them. Keep the size and number of rings and bracelets in proportion to your hand size.

Exercise, for Flexibility and Grace

To stimulate circulation and increase flexibility and gracefulness, try these simple exercises.

TO MAKE HANDS MORE SUPPLE

1. Clench your fingers into a tight fist, then spread them apart as far out and back as you can into an outstretched fan shape. Do both hands simultaneously. Repeat ten times.
2. Tug at each finger of one hand with all the fingers of your other hand as hard as you can. Repeat on the opposite hand.
3. Shake both hands loosely from the wrists as though you were flipping water off of them. Then spread and move your fingers as though you were typing or playing the piano. Repeat five times.

TO FIRM HAND MUSCLES

1. Extend your arms, then open and close your hand as fast and as long as you can without tiring.
2. Pick up a page from a newspaper, holding it by one edge. Using finger and hand muscles only,

roll up the page into a tight roll. Continue with successive pages. You'll feel your muscles strengthen. Repeat with the other hand.

A final word: Never use your nails to scrape, slit, dig, pry, or dial. Treat them like the ten precious jewels they are and they'll ornament your every gesture.

Your Feet Need Special Care

There must be a direct connection between your feet and your face. Because when your feet hurt, your expression reflects the fact. That's just one reason why it's important to take good care of your feet—who wants to go around with aching feet and a pained look? Another reason is that your feet deserve pampering. Even without trying you probably walk about 18,000 steps a day which is a lot of punishment for feet to endure, especially if they're thrust into tight, hot shoes most of the time.

The human foot is incredibly complex. Your two feet contain fifty-two bones (one fourth of all those in your body), one hundred fourteen ligaments, and thirty-eight muscles. The foot has two main arches: the inner longitudinal arch and the metatarsal arch. Together, they form three weight-bearing points: one at the heel, one at the base of the little toe, and one at the base of the big toe. This tripod formation gives each foot perfect balance. No two feet are alike, and no two arches are the same shape or height. In fact, your own two feet no doubt vary.

There are some five hundred known foot ailments and about ninety-five percent of them can be attributed to two causes: poorly fitting shoes and/or stockings and improper care. But don't always blame shoes for your woes. Obesity can be the culprit, forcing your feet to carry a bigger burden than they should. Hereditary factors, injury, or illness can also bring on foot problems.

Next to shoes that fit properly, the most important rule to follow in a foot-care program is to keep the feet as clean as possible. There are more pores to the square inch on the soles of the feet than anywhere else on the body. And feet get less air than most parts of the body and pick up dust and dirt easily. Bathe them every day in warm, soapy water and after you have dried them thoroughly, apply an emollient cream or lotion. Or dust them with powder. If you have acquired corns, calluses, or any of the other troubles that plague neglected feet, be sure to see a podiatrist.

In spite of all the work they do, feet still need exercise to stay healthy. Proper exercise can help relax your feet and ankles and strengthen muscles. Just wiggling your toes back and forth, rotating your foot at the ankle, or flexing your feet toward you while your legs are extended can help make your feet feel more alive and less like numb weights. Walking is probably the best exercise of all. Going barefoot is a good idea but it should be on the right surfaces—sand, grass, or carpeting—not hard surfaces like cement or gravel.

When You Buy Shoes

Never select a pair of shoes because they're just the right color to go with a new outfit. Choose them because they fit and feel comfortable. A shoe should be wide enough to let the toes lie naturally without being crushed together, and about half an inch longer than the foot. The fit at the heel and instep should be snug enough to keep the shoes from slipping off. Walk around the shoe store to make sure of this: A shoe that feels fine when you're sitting may not be as comfortable when you walk.

It's a good idea to buy new shoes late in the afternoon because feet tend to swell during the day. If your shoes feel comfortable then, they are likely to feel good all the time. Also, have your feet measured every time you buy shoes, especially if you're changing from one style of shoe to another. Feet change; they get longer or wider and you may not have noticed the fact. Don't settle for a larger width or a longer shoe because it feels good in the store. Start wearing them and you may develop a crop of blisters because they slide up and down on your feet.

A nice thing to do for your feet is to change heel heights from time to time. High heels put a strain on both feet and legs when worn for long periods of time. Shoes with low heels distribute your body weight more evenly over the foot and eliminate strain. This doesn't mean that if you're at home most of the day, you can go around in rundown floppy bedroom slippers. That's just about the worst thing you can do—an insult to your feet *and* your appearance!

Too-tight shoes aren't the only things that can cause foot trouble. Stockings should fit correctly, too, or they can bring on bunions, ingrown toenails, and other discomforts. Be sure your hosiery is not restricting your foot movements.

A Perfect Pedicure

Pedicures are merely manicures on a lower level but strangely enough, many women don't bother with them or do their toenails infrequently. We asked several women why they skipped pedicures and got many of the same answers. The most-repeated reasons were: "Nobody will see my feet." "I don't like bending over." "My toenails are funny looking." Not one of these three answers is valid. After all, we see our own toenails and that should be reason enough to keep them looking as well groomed as the rest of us. And bending over has nothing to do with it. Not when you can cross your legs and lift one foot up to knee level. And if *funny looking* means irregularly shaped, a greal deal of that will be changed for the better with regular filing, buffing, and cuticle care.

Here, then, are the steps for a perfect pedicure. (Allow about half an hour for the routine every ten days to two weeks. Toenails grow at a slower rate than fingernails which explains why you can allow a little more time between pedicures than manicures.)

Begin by removing old polish. Then clip your nails straight across, using a heavy-duty nail clipper. File smooth with an emery board, filing in one direction only. No seesawing back and forth. Do not round the nails or dig into the corners of the nails; that's an open invitation to a very painful condition—ingrown nails.

Next, soak your feet in warm soapy water for a few moments. Use a wet pumice stone to smooth out calluses on the bottom of your feet or on any thickened skin areas. Scrub your feet with a natural bristle brush, working under and around the nails.

Dry your feet thoroughly, especially between the toes. Apply a cuticle to the base of the nails with your fingers or a cuticle remover with an orangewood stick wrapped in cotton. Work it gently around the base and sides of the nail, pushing back the cuticle. Never use a metal instrument to do this; you could damage the nail base.

And do not clip nail cuticles unless there's a stubborn shred or two that requires cutting. The cuticle on toenails is extremely delicate; cutting into it could cause infection.

Spread emollient cream or lotion on your hands and massage it gently into the feet, working up over the ankles and down to the toes. Massage each toe separately.

If desired, buff your nails to rev up circulation. In one direction only and for no longer than one minute per nail.

Apply polish as you do for a manicure, first separating the toes with a folded tissue to avoid smears. And there's no question about where to start first: Make it the big toe on each foot and work outward. After a base coat, apply two coats of color (toenails were made for bright reds) plus a sealer. Remember to allow sufficient time for each coat to dry thoroughly.

Finally, clean away any smudges with a cotton-wrapped orangewood stick dipped in polish remover.

Oh, My Aching Feet

CORNS. HAPPEN BECAUSE OF PRESSURE OR FRICTION FROM SHOES. They are built-up layers of dead skin, cone-shaped, with the point facing inward. (It's called the eye.) When this presses on a nerve, it can be extremely painful. When corns are between toes, they are moist and referred to as soft corns. More often corns appear on toe joints and on the sole of the foot. For temporary relief, soak the feet in warm water, soften the hardened areas with lanolin, and apply thin pads or plasters to ease the pressure. The wisest solution: See a podiatrist.

CALLUSES. MUCH THE SAME AS CORNS. The cause is identical—undue pressure brought on by poor-fitting shoes and bad posture. Calluses are more shallow than corns and cover a wider area. Again, soaking the feet to soften the hardened skin and a layer of lamb's wool to ease the pressure will help. But a podiatrist can advise you about the basic trouble and help you ward off more of the same.

BUNIONS. MOST PEOPLE WITH BUNIONS ROLL THEIR ANKLES INWARD WHEN THEY WALK, PLACING HEAVY SIDEWARD PRESSURE AGAINST THE JOINT OF THE BIG TOE WITH EACH STEP. This leads to an enlargement of the joint. You can inherit a tendency toward bun-ions and shoes that fit badly also contribute to the condition. There's little you can do with home remedies for bunions: At the first indication of tenderness or swelling of the bit toe goint, get pro-fessional advice.

PUMP BUMPS. THESE ANNOYING LUMPS THAT SHOW UP AT THE BACK OF THE HEELS ARE A SIGNAL THAT YOUR SHOES DON'T FIT PROPERLY. They are sliding sliding up and down as you walk, and irritating the bursa or small sac of fluid at the back of each heel. High-cut pumps in particular can bring about this condition but slingbacks may also be at fault. Massaging your pump bumps each night with an emollient cream will help diminish them but the important thing is to change shoe styles. Look for a shoe cut high or low enough to miss hitting the bursa. If you don't want to give up those expensive new pumps that started it all, slip a small felt pad beneath the lining of the shoe at the heel to raise your foot so shoe and sensitive area don't meet.

FEET THAT PERSPIRE. ORDINARY TALCUM POWDER WILL WILL HELP BLOT UP THE MOISTURE BUT YOU ARE BETTER OFF USING THE SPECIAL FOOT POWDERS THAT CONTAIN MORE ABSORBENT, ANTISEPTIC AGENTS. All-cotton hosiery or cotton socks will absorb the excess mois-ture much more than your nylon hose can do. Make it a point to bathe your feet daily, dry them carefully, and then powder. Alcohol, applied to the soles of the feet, will help cut down perspiration. And use foot powder inside your shoes. If the condition worsens, by all means talk to your doc-tor about it. It may come from nervous tension or from some physical cause that a doctor can handle best.

INGROWN NAILS. IMPROPER NAIL-CUTTING, TOO SHORT OR TOO NARROW SHOES, AND FOOT IMBALANCE ARE PRIME CAUSES OF THIS PAINFUL CONDITION. Usually it affects the big toe but it can occur on any one of the toes. If the nail has dug into the flesh, you can relieve the pain by easing the pressure. Insert a wisp of cotton under the nail at the corner where it has become "ingrown." Use an orangewood stick or blunt toothpick. There's a real danger that the nail will penetrate the flesh and set up an infection. That's reason enough for you to get professional help as soon as possible.

PLANTAR WARTS. THE TECHNICAL NAME FOR THIS PAINFUL CONDITION IS *verrucae*. What it is, is an ingrowing wart on the foot—usually on the soles of the feet and occasionally on the backs of the heels. Thought to be caused by a virus, plantar warts tend to spread if not treated and may take a long time to clear up. Sometimes surgery is necessary.

Summing Up

Don't blame your feet for all the fatigue and nervousness you may experience; they probably are to blame for part but not all. Keep your feet healthy and keep yourself much more comfortable by sticking to common-sense rules for foot care, including bathing your feet daily; changing shoes and hosiery at least once a day; wearing shoes of the proper size and shape; wearing hosiery half an inch longer than your longest toe; and sitting, standing, and walking properly, and exercising your feet. The best way to do this is by walking. And if some romantic individual comes along and offers to drink champagne out of your slipper at a party some night, tell him he's in luck. He'll do much better than he would have back at the turn of the century when men went around quaffing wine from slippers. The average foot size for a woman's shoe then was size six. Today it's size eight and that means better than ten ounces of champagne!

9 / Winning the Diet Game

Why is it that as you add a few years, things get harder to do? Like hurrying up a flight of stairs, bending over to fix a sandal strap, running to catch a bus—and dieting? It was so easy to do any one of these when you were younger than springtime. But now that autumn has set in, more effort is required. Especially when it comes to dieting.

Think diet and immediately you think of counting calories, a type of arithmetic you dislike. Of course you know that a calorie is a unit of measurement, just like an inch or an ounce. An inch measures distance, an ounce measures weight, and a calorie measures the fuel value of foods. You also know that calories which are not burned as fuel eventually end up as body fat.

But are you aware of the fact that as you grow older, you need fewer calories to stay just as you are? Your BMR (basal metabolism rate: an estimate of the energy the body at rest requires just to keep itself going) slows down as you age; thus you require far fewer calories to maintain your weight.

When you were twenty-one and weighed one hundred ten pounds (ah, remember those willowy days!) you needed eighteen hundred calories a day to stay sylphlike. At forty-five you need about one thousand six hundred fifty calories a day to maintain your weight, whatever it may be. And at sixty-five, fifteen hundred calories are all you require. Obviously, if you continue to consume the same number of calories as you have been doing in previous years, the extra calories will be stored up as excess body fat and you'll be wondering why your skirt zipper won't zip up anymore.

There's only one tried-and-true formula for slenderizing. It goes like this: Eat less. Eat fewer high calorie foods. Expend more energy. Diet experts have figured out that it takes eating only about fifteen calories a day to maintain each pound you weigh. But it takes *not* eating thirty-five hundred calories to lose just one of those pounds. (The ratio never changes: thirty-five hundred calories equal one pound.)

You may think it unfair that at any age it still takes that thirty-five hundred-calorie deficit to lose a single pound. Even though you've reached the point when it takes fewer calories to stay put. But consider this low blow from Mother Nature: As you grow older, you're likely to gain weight, not lose it. Certainly you'll get "fatter." Bodywise at twenty-one, you are about twenty-six-percent fat; by age fifty-five, you'll be more like thirty-eight-percent fat, even if you weigh exactly the same. As your body gradually changes into more fat and less muscle, you can't avoid looking as though you weigh more—even if you don't.

But here's cheerier news: The more you weigh, the more you are able to lose through exercise. A woman weighing one hundred fifty pounds, for example, who plays tennis with a woman weighing one hundred twenty-five pounds, will burn up more calories in the same amount of time than her partner does.

If the prospect of going on a diet sends you into a panic, something is wrong. A diet doesn't have to mean skimpy meals, hunger pangs, and boredom. If that's how you feel, you need a new viewpoint on dieting as much as you need a new waistline. Dieting means eating the right foods instead of the wrong ones. It means wholesome, balanced, and interesting meals drawn from the entire span of basic food groups, not just from one or two of them. And it should never mean restricting yourself to some strange combination of foods, like bananas and veal chops. You may lose weight on a fad diet but it will probably be no more than a loss of water. Give up those bananas and veal chops and the indicator on your bathroom scale will whip right back to your former weight in no time.

Any meaningful diet is bound to bring some changes into your life. You are going to have to acquire new eating habits and you can't afford to backslide into your old careless ones. You'll be able to eat many of the foods you've been accustomed to eating—but in smaller portions and prepared differently. Also, you are going to have to be more active. Watching what you eat is only part of the slimming battle. As the pounds slide off, you'll need to exercise more to keep your muscles firm and to increase your physical energy. Diet and exercise combined are the basic tools to help you achieve and maintain good health, vitality, and an attractive figure. You can't do one and ignore the other.

Motivation Counts Most

No diet is going to be a success unless the dieter is properly motivated. Every successful diet begins in the mind. You must have a reason to want to lose weight, a reason so powerful, so important to you, that nothing will make you waver in your resolve to get rid of those bumps and bulges. Perhaps you are starting a new job and can't bear the thought of being the only size eighteen in a sea of size nines. Or your husband came home from the office and said with obvious admiration, "My new secretary is a little slip of a thing!" Or suddenly you can't even squeeze into your favorite designer swimsuit. Or at your last checkup, your doctor mentioned something about high blood pressure being associated with obesity. Whatever the reason that prompts you to begin dieting, be sure it's strong enough to keep you going. You've got to want to lose and keep wanting to lose if you're ever going to lose.

Preparing for a diet is also a good way to insure that it will work. Do some advance homework, particularly on nutrition. Review the four food groups—milk, meat, vegetable-fruit, and bread-cereal—and the recommended daily servings from each. Know which foods are low in calories and which are high in nutritive value. Learn the protein-giving foods—milk, meat, poultry, fish, eggs, and cheese. And the foods that are rich in minerals and vitamins—cereals, many raw and cooked vegetables, and fruits. All foods have some caloric content but the greatest sources are in fats—fat meat, butter, margarine, shortening, cream, salad oil, and in sugary, starchy foods. (These are going to be foods you must cut down on.)

Most important, analyze your present eating habits. Get yourself a notebook and for one whole week before you begin dieting, record everything you eat and add the time, the circumstances, and your mood or feeling. Do you eat more when you are bored, restless, depressed, and upset? Are you an in-between meals nibbler? Do you dote on sweets and rich desserts? Do you pile on the calories at the cocktail hour? Must you always have a midnight snack? The record you've kept for a week will give you a clear picture of how you relate to food and how you are using it to satisfy certain emotional needs as well as nutritional ones. Also, you'll have clear evidence at hand if you've been eating too many starchy, sweet, fatty, or salty foods, the ones that increase weight. Ounce for ounce, they contain more calories than nonstarch foods like vegtables, fruits, seafood, and poultry.

Keep a record as well of your activities during your prediet week. You may be amazed at the amount of time you spend sitting at a desk, in front of the television set, or at the dining table. Plan to be more active while you're dieting. You can lose weight on a diet, but if you combine exercise with diet, your figure will look trimmer and firmer and your body proportions will improve. Besides, exercise burns up extra calories.

Use Common Sense to Diet

There are many established "name diets" that can help you lose weight. You may have tried some of them already but your motivation may have been weak and you gave up too soon. Or you lost weight and then went right back to your old eating habits in celebration of the fact! You really don't need a set formula to lose weight; you do need common sense. The key to weight reduction and maintenance is the enjoyment of a variety of good foods, but not too much of any one. Start out by choosing only foods from the basic food groups. The recommended servings each day are two from the milk group, four or more from the vegetable-fruit group, two or more from the meat group; and two or three from the bread-cereal group. Remember, the proportion of each food is important.

It's vital that you reduce your fat intake. The effective way to accomplish this is to eat only lean meats and limit your meat intake. (Remove all visible fat before cooking.) Eat more poultry, with the exception of duck and goose. Eat more fish. Prepare foods by baking and broiling and eliminate fried foods. Avoid or use sparingly, butter, whole milk, and whole milk products. Substitute skim milk, cottage cheese, and margarine made from polyunsaturated fats. Use liquid oil shortenings or margarine made from polyunsaturated fats for cooking. Cut down on, or eliminate, bakery products and pastries because they usually are high in saturated fats.

High fiber foods play a vital role in weight reduction because they provide "bulk" and thus give a feeling of fullness. Reduce or eliminate refined foods, processed white flour products, and high starch foods. Eat whole grain cereal products and whole grain breads. Eat high fiber fruits and vegetables, raw if possible, including cabbage, cauliflower, berries, carrots, apples, figs, and dark greens.

If you're more comfortable on a diet when you have a specific calorie count to cling to, limit your food intake to approximately 1,200 calories a day. It's probably about 1,000 less than you are now eating.

Don't be impatient. Having checked with your doctor and decided on the number of pounds you can safely lose, don't try to lose them overnight. Take it slow and easy. For example, if you have decided to lose a total of thirty-five pounds, you might try to lose half of this amount over a period of two to three months. If you shed about two pounds a week, your body will have a better chance at adjusting gradually to the change. And you'll feel better, not fatigued.

More Diet Tips

Learn to love water; it's calorie free and a great appetite-cutter. Drink an eight-ounce glass before every meal. Drink low calorie beverages occasionally. Drink coffee black and tea without sugar.

Don't skip meals; eat three balanced meals each day at a regular hour. Remember, permanent weight loss involves retraining your poor eating habits. If you skip breakfast or live on snacks during the day with a main meal at night, you've got to reform or you're dieting in vain.

Do sit down for meals, eat slowly, chew food thoroughly, and put down your fork between bites. All this helps you to feel satisfied with less food. (More than eighty percent of overweight people are fast eaters who often stand up while they eat.)

Weigh yourself once a week; don't think you must get on the scale every single day. It could unnerve you if you reach a standstill. And that happens to almost every dieter when lost fat is temporarily replaced with water in the tissues—a condition that gradually corrects itself as you continue to diet. Always weigh yourself at the same hour in the morning before breakfast and without clothing. As you get closer to your ideal weight, you'll notice that your weight loss is less dramatic— don't fret. It means you're getting there!

For encouragement and inspiration, many women go out and buy a new outfit, a size or two smaller than what they're presently wearing as a prod but this can be expensive. Keeping a "wish-I-were-that-skinny photograph" taped to the refrigerator door can be just as effective and a lot cheaper.

Don't forget to eat a raw fruit and/or vegetable daily. If you get hungry between meals, drink a cup of bouillon or tomato juice or nibble on low calorie snacks of raw vegetables.

Don't tell everyone that you're on a diet. You'll do better if you keep the news to yourself because then you'll be under less pressure to show instant results. Besides, few people are really interested in diets, especially when they're not on one and should be.

Finally, don't get discouraged if you weaken and go off your diet. Chalk it up to experience and get back to your diet routine with more determination than ever. But concern yourself only with today; let tomorrow take care of itself. In other words, control your diet one day at a time. You're the only one who can create that new slimmer you and it's going to take persistence. After a few weeks of firmly saying, "No, thank you" to the pasta and chocolate cream pie, you'll not only feel proud of yourself, but you'll feel thinner. It's a delightful feeling!

DESIRABLE WEIGHTS FOR WOMEN*

Height		Small Frame	Medium Frame	Large Frame
Feet	Inches			
4	10	102-111	109-121	118-131
4	11	103-113	111-123	120-134
5	0	104-115	113-126	122-137
5	1	106-118	115-129	125-140
5	2	108-121	118-132	128-143
5	3	111-124	121-135	131-147
5	4	114-127	124-138	134-151
5	5	117-130	127-141	137-155
5	6	120-133	130-144	140-159
5	7	123-136	133-147	143-163
5	8	126-139	136-150	146-167
5	9	129-142	139-153	149-170
5	10	132-145	142-156	152-173
5	11	135-148	145-159	155-176
6	0	138-151	148-162	158-179

*Source: Metropolitan Life Insurance Company
Weights at ages 25-59 based on lowest mortality.
Weight in pounds according to frame (in indoor clothing weighing 3 pounds, shoes with 1-inch heels).

10 / Body Shaping

If you're fortyish, out of shape, and if doing anything more than using a touch telephone exhausts you, you probably don't want to hear about exercise. But it's one subject you can't afford to ignore, especially if you are anxious to improve your appearance and feel younger and more fit.

Is exercise necessary?

One physical fitness expert puts it this way.

Go home, take off your clothes, stand in front of a full-length mirror, and look at yourself. If you see a body which is slender and supple; if the skin is glowing, the muscles firm; if there are no bulges or awkward angles showing; if your bust, waist, and hips are in perfect proportion; your breathing deep and rhythmic; your movements flexible; then it may be you can do without exercise—for twenty-four hours.

It's difficult to understand why exercise has earned such a bad name for itself, particularly among people who may never have tried it or who spend their days avoiding it. The truth is, you can't say enough good things about exercise.

For example, with exercise you can actually redesign your body. You can pare down your hips or slim your waistline; build up your bosom; or reshape your thighs. Exercise perfects posture which in turn makes any outfit you put on look better.

Exercise improves your breath control and your endurance. And restores flexibility to stiff muscles. So look for a change if you currently puff your way up a flight of stairs or wince when you bend over to pick up something you've dropped.

Exercise breeds energy; you'll have more and spend less on any given task. An unfit body is only twenty-seven-percent energy-efficient. Regular exercise doubles this rate, so count on doubling your work capacity.

It's not necessarily true that if you exercise, you eat more and thus cancel out the good results of a diet. Actually, exercise can curb the appetite—blood sugar doesn't fluctuate so much after exercise, thus keeping hunger away longer. In fact, exercise improves digestion and makes you less irritable and edgy if you are on a reducing diet. And don't worry that exercise will help turn you into a "Fat Lady"; it builds muscle definition, not bulges.

Exercise is preventive medicine; it helps your body fight disease, stimulates circulation, increases sweat, and reduces body salt. Studies show that lowering salt levels in the brain can actually improve your mood. Ergo, exercise and stay happier.

Exercise does away with the need for sleeping pills because it acts as a natural tranquilizer and increases deep sleep. And here's one more welcome plus: Exercise speeds up your metabolic rate and keeps it up for about six hours after a workout. Thus, calories burn up even while you're taking it easy.

So don't ask, "Is exercise necessary?" The real question is, "How can anyone afford not to exercise?"

How to Get Started

Just as we advise about dieting, we suggest that you do some homework first to reacquaint yourself with the subject of exercise and wipe out any negative feelings you may have toward it. Walk or jog to your nearest bookstore or library and get an armful of background reading. You're going to discover that there's a lot more to exercise than toe touches and leg lifts. In fact, you may be overwhelmed at first at the variety of exercises. And the different kinds of exercise—plain old-fashioned calisthenics. Yoga. Hathayoga. Aerobics. Isometrics or muscle tensing. Walking, running, jogging, and bicycling. See? You're already into your fitness program! Sports like tennis, racquetball, golf, and riding. And don't forget dancing, the pleasurable way to go.

Spurred on by those before-and-after pictures in some of your exercise tomes, you'll doubtless resolve to start on your own program of calisthenics right away. Then come the questions of when and where. When is easy. There are twenty-four hours in a day and you can exercise during any of them—morning, noon, or night. It's all a matter of personal preference. "Where" calls for a debate. There's nothing wrong with doing your exercises right at home. But give some serious consideration to joining an exercise group. Almost every community has a health center, spa, or club where you'll be able to get the benefit of professional advice on fitness and workout in a class. When you're out of shape, misery and company make magnificent companions. There's nothing as comforting as stepping into a roomful of women in droopy gray sweat pants and realizing you are not alone. Even more comforting is to realize that your sweat pants are a size smaller than most. By the time you all graduate to leotards and slimmer figures, you are bosom companions. Also, a health center can provide scientific exercise equipment, steam rooms, saunas, a swimming pool, and other facilities to help speed you on to a shapelier self.

However, if you do prefer to confine your bending and stretching to home territory, Suzy Prudden, one of the nation's leading fitness experts, suggests you ask a friend or two to join you. Alone, you are tempted to slow down. With a competitive partner or partners, you tend to work out more enthusiastically. Suzy also says you'd be smart to exercise to music. It will give you a better sense of pace and rhythm, make you feel as though you're having fun, not torturing yourself.

That's a misconception about exercise that Ms. Prudden feels strongly about. Exercise is never to be equated with punishment in her book. She believes that too many women shy away from daily exercise or give it up too quickly once they start because they believe exercise routines have to be difficult, almost painful, or they don't count. Not so, says Suzy. You don't have to do one hundred toe touches or two hundred knee bends to prove you're keeping fit. Any movement that limbers and stretches the muscles qualifies. If exercise hurts, it's wrong. You should never feel strained or tired after a session; you should feel invigorated and refreshed.

The Prudden philosophy about fitness begins and ends with this declaration. "You have only one body and it's up to you to keep it healthy by eating properly and exercising regularly. If you exercise seriously, you'll see results in three weeks. In three months, you'll have a new shape!"

According to Suzy, never exercise too long or too strenuously. About twenty minutes a day is sufficient but it must be every day without fail. And don't abandon your calisthenics in the summertime because you're outdoors a lot, swimming, playing tennis, or jogging. Sports are great but they may not give you the specific help you need and that regular exercising can give you. For example, exercise helps tighten up flabby underarms and inner thighs. Sports activities may not.

Stretching Counts Too

You don't always have to be formal about exercise. Floor mats, chin bars, or stationary bicycles are not *de rigueur.* You don't even have to get down on the floor and extend your arms and legs in dramatic moves. In the course of a day you have many opportunities to exercise quietly and effectively in little ways that no one may notice unless you call attention to the fact. You can do "hidden exercises" while you're sitting at a desk, waiting for a bus, standing in a supermarket line— whenever you have a few moments to yourself. These are the muscle-tensing exercises that require no sweeping moves. Exercise, too, while you're doing housework or going up and down the stairs or standing or walking— just by keeping your posture correct, with your body aligned and your muscles under control.

Just plain old-fashioned stretching can be extremely effective. In the morning when you awaken, pretend your body is an elastic band and stretch it as you lie in bed. Stretch one side up, the other down; then reverse the procedure. Occasionally during the day stretch tall, lifting your neck and head high as if you were trying to push right through the ceiling. Or stand in a doorway and stretch both arms up to reach above the door opening. If you sit for long periods of time, interrupt your work once in a while for a big, overall body stretch. Raise your arms high and stretch until you feel your waist muscles tighten. Or when you're sitting in a chair, extend your legs and stretch them as far out as you can, then drop them back down.

After a tiring day, try the rag doll slump. Just stand with your feet apart and bend over from your hips until your head, neck, and arms are hanging loosely. Now swing slowly from side to side as though you were a rag doll. Hang lower and lower from the waist until your fingers finally touch the floor. Just dangle there and swing back and forth eight or ten times. It's an easy, effective way to revivify circulation and relax tense muscles. (And surprise anyone who comes in the room and catches you.)

The theory behind isometrics or muscle tensing is that it strengthens muscles that have grown slack and lazy. If you contract a muscle to the maximum, as hard as you can and hold it that way for seconds, the muscle becomes six percent stronger in a week, sixty percent stronger in ten weeks. Muscle tensing can help improve almost any part of the body. You'll discover that abdominal muscles show dramatic results very quickly once you practice muscle tensing. All you have to do is pull in your stomach as hard as possible, so hard that you can feel the muscles quiver. Then relax. Do this tummy tensing before you get out of bed in the morning and frequently during the day. Before long your stomach is going to look much flatter and that's flattering!

Some Traditional Spot Reducers

A word of advice before you begin your exercise program! Don't regard it merely as a way to whittle down your waistline and thighs. It probably will accomplish this but do keep in mind that your real goal is to have a body that is fit, graceful, and disciplined. Exercising properly and regularly should mean as much to your self-improvement regimen as skin care and dieting. Never do exercises automatically, thinking of something else all the while. You must control each movement with your mind for maximum results. Wear comfortable clothing and a minimum of it, never anything that might hinder the freedom of your movements. By the way, if your body has a great deal of flabby fat, you may be happy to know that with exercise, soft fat may break up more quickly than solid, hard fat. Those who have solid fat on their bodies will need to break up the fat deposits with a combination of diet and exercise. When they begin to lose weight and their measurements decrease, they will notice that as the fat breaks up, it gradually softens before it goes away. But keep on exercising and eventually your body will grow firm.

There are literally dozens of exercises for overweight, ungainly figures. Here are just a few selected to "hit the spot." Do them faithfully and you should see results in as little as two weeks' time.

FOR THE BUST

Stand erect, extend the arms and close the fists tightly. Raise the arms to shoulder height, then push them forward and backward 10 times. With the arms still extended, follow this by pushing the arms out sideways, then back in, the fists touching the chest— back and forth 10 times. Finally, place your hands on your shoulders and draw large circles in the air with your elbows, first backward, then forward. Again, 10 times to start; increase the count as you grow more proficient.

FOR YOUR SHOULDERS, BACK, AND ABDOMEN

Sit on the floor, your legs straight and apart, your hands clasped behind your neck. Keep your elbows back. Now bend and swing to touch your head to your right knee. Resume an upright position and repeat, this time touching your left knee. Repeat 10 times.

FOR YOUR TORSO AND WAISTLINE

Stand erect, your feet slightly apart. Stretch your arms above your head, your hands clasped. Bending from the waist, stretch your arms first to the far left side, then above your head and over to the far right side. Do this with rhythmic motion, twisting your waist from side to side as you go. Work up to 20 times.

TO REDUCE YOUR ABDOMEN

Lie down on the floor with folded towels under your hips. Extend your arms at shoulder level, palms up. Bend both knees over your chest. Clasp your hands around your left knee and pull your leg toward your chest. Straighten your right leg up toward the ceiling, and pulling your stomach in tightly, lower your right leg toward the floor but lower it only to hip level, never all the way to the floor. Hold. Return to your starting position. Raise your left leg and repeat. Repeat 8 times. (Difficult at first but well worth the effort.)

FOR FATTY KNEES

Lie on your back, your legs together, your hands clasped behind your neck. Raise your right leg; point your toe; stiffen your knee. At a 45-degree angle, draw circles in the air with your toe. Do 6 times with one leg; 6 with the other.

TO REDUCE UPPER HIPS

Sit on your right hip, your right leg bent under. Your right arm should be stretched out from the shoulder, your hand flat on the floor. Your top leg is straight and slightly forward. Now rise up on your right knee and stretch your left arm over your body. Stretch 3 times with a bouncy movement. Then sit back again on your hip. Bring your right hand to your left foot. Stretch your left arm behind your back. Bend forward with a bouncy movement 3 times. Repeat 8 times. Then do the exercise 8 times sitting on your left hip.

TO TRIM YOUR HIPS AND THIGHS

Lie on one side, your head resting on your underneath arm, your top arm bent, your hand on the floor near your chest. Raise your top leg up as high as you can; then lower it. Repeat 10 times. Keep your body in a straight, stretched line; don't bend in the middle. Turn to the other side. Repeat 10 lifts with your other leg. This exercise helps side muscles that are seldom used.

FOR YOUR LOWER BACK, ABDOMEN, AND TORSO

Lie on your back, your lower back pressed against the floor. Don't let it arch. Keep your arms stretched along the floor above your head. In a smooth, continuous motion, slowly roll forward and reach to touch your toes. Don't let your feet come up off the floor. Roll back down the same way. Try to feel as though you are moving each section of your spine separately. Repeat 10 times. Sit-ups strengthen your lower back, abdomen, and trunk muscles; keep your abdomen flat and firm; improve your posture and give you all the benefits of stretching.

FOR FIRMING BUTTOCKS

Lie on your stomach, your arms stretched out in front. Lift your chest and legs up as high as you can; hold; then relax. Repeat 10 times. Difficult at first but great for your back, arms, shoulders, and for firm buttocks.

TO REDUCE ANKLES

Lie on the floor with two towels folded and placed under your lower hips. Extend your arms at shoulder level, palms up. Bend your knees over your chest. Straighten one leg up toward the ceiling. Bring this leg toward the floor; then start your other leg toward the ceiling as you bend and bring your first leg back over your chest. Movements should simulate the pedaling of a bicycle. As your legs move, flex the foot of your raised leg; point the toe of the bent leg. Do the exercise until your ankles get tired. Keep your legs up over your chest; don't let them drop all the way to the floor.

Faces Need Exercise, Too

Exercising your face may not have occurred to you but those fifty-five underlying muscles can get slack if you neglect them entirely. Facial exercises tend to make you look peculiar, to say the least, so it's best to do them when privacy surrounds you. Here's an easy trio for firming facial contours. Do them ten to twenty times each. Puff out your cheeks, open your lips slightly, and make believe you're blowing at a feather placed at nose level. Move your jaws as if you were chewing gum in an exaggerated manner. Open your mouth wide, drop your jaw, then close your mouth with a firm, quick motion.

And here's a simple wake-up exercise that will do wonders for double chins and slack necks. Before getting out of bed, lie faceup and let your head hang over the edge of the bed. Lift your head and let it drop back several times. This strengthens the chin muscles, relaxes neck tension, and tones up the complexion because blood is circulating rapidly to your head.

Make the Outdoors Your Gym

Sports activities are an exciting, challenging, even ego-boosting way to improve your body and your health. You'll lose weight in some of the most satisfying places, have more energy, and gain a marvelous sense of well-being that, intangible though it is, may just be the greatest reward of all.

Take swimming. True, it shows off the most of your figure (something fatties hate) but it also does the most for it. As a body shaper, it has no equal. Swim and every inch of you gets a workout.

Here's an estimate of how many calories a 115-pound woman burns up when swimming, depending on the stroke she uses and how fast she swims: backstroke, 220 to 445 calories per hour; sidestroke, 390 per hour; crawl, 225 to 498 calories per hour; and butterfly, about 547 calories per hour. Regardless of the strokes you use, remember: Swimming constantly stretches the waist muscles. You'll seldom see a thick waistline on a dedicated swimmer. That should be enough to make you take the plunge!

Tennis, golf, volleyball—they're all guaranteed figure trimmers. Tennis, especially singles, gives you a real workout. It trims down bulges, increases stamina and muscle coordination, and burns off calories (about 325 to 455 per hour depending on how hard you play). Back and waist muscles are stretched in the serves as well as with forehand and backhand shots; and those lateral movements benefit the thighs and buttocks. Even as you run and grip the ground with the toes to stop, you're exercising. It helps calf muscles. Golf improves your posture and the arms and legs—all that swinging and walking. And any type of ball game, played vigorously, will improve your coordination and strengthen your arm, back, and leg muscles.

You'll never be bored when you exercise by horseback riding. Properly done, riding is a marvelous aid to good posture and is especially effective for leg muscles. As you move with the horse, your hips and buttocks get a workout. And controlling the reins means hand and arm benefits.

Bicycling is another appealing way to melt pounds off your hips and thighs. Experts suggest five to ten miles of cycling at an even pace, at least three times a week, to keep you in shape. As you ride, you constantly exercise your chest, back, and stomach muscles, as well as your arms and legs. And since you're expanding your lungs and taking in oxygen all the while, your circulation is revved up—a plus for your complexion. Of course, if you're shy about cycling along roadsides, you can always use an at-home exercycle. The views may be limited but the benefits won't be.

Running and jogging also are excellent ways to exercise—your body, lungs, and heart all benefit. But it's important to keep a constant pace. In jogging especially, don't pound your heels down on the ground— that's the sure way to tendon damage. And wear proper shoes for the task. You may want to begin your "roadwork" by taking a brisk walk, alone or with a friend. The fact is, you can lose ten pounds a year simply by walking one mile a day, as long as your caloric intake remains about the same. Start with ten minutes of slow-paced walking and gradually work up to half an hour at a brisk pace, twice a day if you can. A good pace is about three or three and a half miles an hour. Don't push yourself too hard. If you feel tired or your muscles tighten up, stop. Remember, the object of any walking program is to build up unused muscles *gradually*. If you feel warmed up and glowing after fifteen minutes of brisk walking, you're doing all right.

Indoors, there's bowling (great for your arms, legs, and back) and table tennis (equally kind to your arms, legs, and waistline). Dancing does wonders for your whole figure, not to mention what it can do for your sense of balance and grace. Take a ballet, tap, or jazz class. Join a folk-dancing group. Or do-si-do at a weekly square dance. It's going to be fun. It's going to help improve your figure. And it's definitely going to banish any self-destructive, middle-aged thoughts you've been brooding about.

Activity	Energy Cost in Calories Per Hour
Rest and Light Activity	50–200
Lying down or sleeping	80
Sitting	100
Driving an automobile	120
Standing	140
Doing household chores	180
Moderate Activity	200–350
Bicycling (5½ mph)	210
Walking (2½ mph)	210
Gardening	220
Golf	250
Bowling	270
Rowing (2½ mph)	300
Swimming (¼ mph)	300
Horseback riding (trotting)	350
Square dancing	350
Vigorous Activity	over 350
Playing table tennis	360
Skating (10 mph)	400
Tennis	420
Waterskiing	480
Skiing (10 mph)	600
Running (10 mph)	900

Source: American Medical Association and the President's Council on Physical Fitness and Sports.

Check First

Every wonder why the experts always say: See your doctor before you embark on an exercise program? It's not alarmist. In your enthusiasm and desire to slim down in record time you may pick exercises that are not suitable for your body. The back, for example, is especially vulnerable. And one of the most popular slim-down exercises is that oldie suggesting that you lift both straightened legs at once while lying on your back.

Sit-ups with the knees bent and the feet stabilized is another. So before you get started on the way to a muscular problem all the while you're slimming and trimming, do talk to your doctor. He or she can test you for limberness and provide you with helpful observations on the kind of stretches and bends that suit you best.

11 / How Young Is Your Personality?

Some time ago, a book titled *Think Yourself Thin* became an overnight best-seller. Its premise: Concentrate on a conviction that you're losing weight and the pounds will drop off. The system worked for a lot of readers, possibly because it made them so conscious of food and calories that they eased up on eating.

A book called *Think Yourself Young* would no doubt have equal success—because no cosmetic, no exercise, no new hairstyle, hair color, or smashing outfit can help you look younger more effectively than your mind can. Think young and you'll find yourself acting young, feeling young, and looking young. On the other hand, think old and you won't need a birth certificate to establish your maturity. Your attitude will tell it to the world.

The dictionary defines personality as "the sum total of individual, behavioral, and emotional tendencies, something evidenced by distinguishing character traits, attitudes, or habits." It doesn't distinguish between young and old personalities but it hardly needs to. You're undoubtedly familiar with both types. Wherever you go, you're bound to meet them—at the office, in school, in stores, and even right at home. They're instantly recognizable. The youthful personality is usually friendly, tolerant, positive, and open to new ideas. The "old" personality is apt to be negative, critical, impatient, and inflexible...acid qualities, all, that tend to etch ugly lines in a face.

Youth is eternally linked with sparkle, gaiety, enthusiasm, and love. If you're seriously dedicated to creating a new, younger image for yourself—and you must be, or you wouldn't have read this far—ask yourself if you have made a conscious effort to retain those bright and upbeat attitudes. Or have you gradually let yourself slip into a nagging, irritable state of mind and cranky, unpleasant ways?

It's easy to let aging attitudes sneak up on you if you're not paying careful attention. All too soon, those attitudes turn into aging habits or mannerisms that establish your image for others.

If you got out of bed this morning, scowled in the mirror, wrapped yourself in a shabby robe, shuffled downstairs, and yawned your way through breakfast, grumbling about the weather and your job, you're playing the "old game."

If you smiled in the mirror, put on a pretty robe, hurried down to breakfast, chatted happily about the day's plans, that's acting young, moving young, and consequently, looking young.

At the office you turn down an opportunity for advancement because you "don't know how to analyze a computer readout and it's too late to learn." That's old. Or you organize a lunchtime exercise class. That's young.

On your vacation, you go back to the same resort you've summered at for the past five years. You don't like the place that much but it's familiar and comfortable. That's old. Or you join a community travel group and start planning a trip to China. That's young.

Some Think-Young Formulas

We canvassed a few forty-plus women who have made it a point to stay youthful. Their comments should inspire other middle-agers to go and do likewise.

AN ACTRESS. I think young; I simply never think of myself as getting older. Years ago, I decided that I would pick a favorite age and stay with it. I picked twenty-nine because it was one of my happiest years. I looked well, felt well, and enjoyed life then. And I still do, thanks to my convictions.

A WRITER. Self-confidence is an important element in the think-and-stay-young routine. You can't look at yourself and say, "Mirror, mirror on the wall, I'm the dreariest of them all." You have to think positively, forget the encroaching wrinkles, and be grateful for your abundant hair or your slender hands.

A TEACHER. One habit that practially guarantees the years will never show is putting others first. Forget yourself and dwell on what's around you. Listen to, look at, and think about, others. That way you don't have a chance to brood about yourself.

A FASHION DESIGNER. To look young at any age, you must keep physically fit. Exercise, diet, have regular facials, haircuts, and coloring. And besides discipline for the body, you have to create a youthful image via your wardrobe. If you fear getting old and losing your looks and health, you could be losing them while you worry. Follow the principles of good health and be confident. With confidence comes vitality and with vitality, youthfulness. I believe when a woman's age shows these days, it is strictly from neglect.

An Attitude Quiz

Here's a quick test to help you determine if you're letting your attitudes age you. Three yeses and you had better start renovating your ideas about yourself and others. Five and you're headed for trouble. Over five, better do a complete revamping of attitudes if you want to stay as youthful as possible.

1. Do you resent others being cheerful around you when you're not feeling that way?
2. Do you make an effort to talk to others or do you wait for them to speak to you?
3. Do you get upset when someone unexpectedly drops in to visit you?
4. Are you intolerant of others' mistakes?
5. Has it been quite a while since you've read a best-seller?
6. Are you unable to identify any of the current popular songs?
7. When you go to a party, do you secretly yearn to get home and get out of your dress-up clothes?
8. Do you avoid making new friends, especially among those younger than yourself?
9. Do you think many current fashions are too extreme?
10. In conversations, do you often say, "I remember when...?"

What Mannerisms Reveal

So you tore out the page in the family Bible that recorded your birthdate, hid your birth certificate, spilled ink on your passport, and folded your driver's license so that the crease falls on the line stating your age. It's no use—you can't hide your age from the rest of the world—not as long as you have certain mannerisms or habits that say "old!"

A great many of these mannerisms or habits have to do with body movement. For example, could it be that you're "running old"? The next time you have to make a dash for a cab or bus, pay attention to the way you run. Do you hold your head forward and down, grimly hang onto your hat, bundles, and umbrella with one arm, and flay the air stiffly with the other as you propel yourself forward, doing something excessively awkward with your legs? True, the older you get, the stiffer your body becomes and the harder it is to run gracefully. But if you keep your body limber with exercise and give some thought to the way you move, you can eliminate much of that aging awkwardness. Study the way young people move—they literally flow along, heads up, arms and legs loose and limber. No one expects you to become a teenage gazelle but do make an effort to limber up your running style. If you can't and feel you're always going to wind up looking awkward and breathless, better drop track from your life. There's always another bus.

We've talked about the importance of good posture and the need to walk and sit gracefully if you are going to present a vital, youthful-looking image to the world in an earlier chapter. We won't repeat the guidelines but we do want to impress again on you how loudly the way you walk or sit can tattle on your age. You could be twice as old as you admit but a lively, brisk way of walking will never betray the fact. Slouch along indifferently or walk as though every step were agony and you're doubling your age.

One thing an actress does when she wants to portray an older woman is to take teetering, wobbly little steps. If you're in the habit of teetering along, you may be wearing the wrong shoes or neglecting to care for your feet properly. There are exercises to strengthen weak ankles so you don't really have to go around wavering as you walk. And in addition to changing your shoe style, change your attitude about walking. Walk easily and firmly, as though you were headed for someplace you want very much to reach—it will make a definite improvement in your appearance.

We have already talked about grimaces, too, and

how they can add wrinkles and age to your face. Grimacing is another one of those unconscious habits that have a negative effect on your image. Sit down in front of a mirror and go through all your favorite frowns and twitches so that you can see how unattractive you look. Ask a friend to give you a high sign every time he catches you grimacing. And make an effort to pin a smile on your mind every morning and leave it there all day—pleasant thoughts wind up as pleasant expressions.

Any time you let your body act and look as though it were encased in cement, you are destroying the illusion of youngness. Getting in and out of cars is a prime example. Some women back in; some tumble in; some get half in but their legs and feet won't follow and they have to get out to try all over again. It's the perfect way to give an impression of awkward uncertainty.

If you want to improve your car-entry style, know that the secret lies in the approach. You stand gracefully erect beside the open door of the car, facing front. Keep both legs together, feet forward. Then, in a quick, smooth movement, bend your body toward the car as though you were going to sit down sideways (which you are). As you do, use a slide-in motion to put your body into the car seat, quickly swing both legs up and into the car together, not so far apart that one leg is in and the other dangling curbside. That's the way models in car ads do it—and it always looks beautiful.

Here are some other age-tattling mannerisms you may have acquired without knowing it. None of them are very serious—you can get by with them, especially if you have so much charm in other ways that people allow you a few idiosyncrasies. But why give yourself an "old look" unnecessarily? Stop and think of the way you put on a coat or jacket in a restaurant, for example. When someone offers to help you on with your coat, do you turn into a kind of windmill or threshing machine, arms waving in the air, never quite connecting with the coat sleeves? Don't let a simple thing like slipping into a coat become a demonstration of how arthritic or astigmatic you've become.

And if you wear eyeglasses, have you fallen into the habit of identifying them with the passage of years—out loud? Four out of five women will make some gratuitous remark whenever they have to put on glasses. Looking at a menu, reading a newspaper, or selecting a book—out will come the glasses and the owner will say apologetically, "Can't see a thing without them!" Everyone knows what glasses are for, including all the children and teenagers who wear them. Why constantly relate them to aging?

And if you're not convinced by now that habits or mannerisms are real hazards to any I-would-look-young program, consider The Clutcher, The Patter, and The Toter.

Perhaps it's because the older we get, the more suspicious we become but too many women get into the habit of clutching their handbags in an "it's all mine" manner. We don't suggest you proffer your purse to passing pickpockets. But it is entirely possible to carry a handbag gracefully and securely at the same time. You'll see when you practice in front of your mirror. Clutching is like wincing—it looks tense and old.

The Patter is not as suspicious as The Clutcher but she's very insecure. And uncertainty is another big giveaway of passing years. The Patter feels so unsure of herself that she keeps patting her hair, shifting her neckline, pulling at her necklace, and dabbing her face with little wads of tissue all day long. Don't be a patter. It totally destroys that charming, self-assured look you're striving to maintain.

Toters are everywhere these days because tote bags and shopping bags have become a way of life. But if you're sincerely trying to present a youthful, vital image, leave yours at home. Naturally there are times when you have to carry things—groceries to the car, for example. Or flowers home from the flower stand on the corner.

But we're urging that you try not to be a constant carrier—always lugging around a shopping bag filled to the brim. It not only ruins the posture but it gives a kind of Mother Hubbard look to your appearance. As you know, Mother Hubbard was far from the epitome of chic.

Conversational Mannerisms

Another way to hang cobwebs on the image you present to the public is to talk yourself out of a pleasing personality. We don't mean the tone of your voice—we're coming to that very soon. What we mean is that unconsciously you may have certain conversational mannerisms that say "old" rather than "young." Perhaps the best way to explain this to you is to give you a brief quiz.

1. Do you rush up to people and start talking, indifferent to the fact that they may be busy or have other inclinations?
2. Do you act flustered when someone pays you a compliment?
3. Do you lean in on people, touching them or fussing with their clothes or jewelry while you talk to them?
4. Do you talk a lot about yourself and your achievements?
5. Do you overdo flattery when you're paying a compliment so that the person feels uncomfortable at your fulsomeness?
6. Do you wave your hands and make annoying gestures as you talk?
7. Do you overload your conversation with gloom, linking every topic to disappointment, criticism, and failure?
8. Are you a gossip collector and repeater?
9. Do you use personal problems as a kind of

social blackmail for special attention and sympathy?

10. Are you a constant name-dropper or conversation topper?

A majority of yeses would indicate that you should revamp your social approach; you're not projecting a pleasing personality. A majority of nos and you can rejoice—you're welcome at any gathering.

How Do You Sound?

Most women give a great deal of thought to improving their looks—their hair, faces, figures, and clothes—but they seldom think of improving their voices. And yet one's voice provides a definite clue to age and personality.

How you say something is as important as what you say. If your voice is clear, warm, and melodious, you make a good impression. But open your mouth and speak in a voice that is nasal, shrill, or harsh; and mumble, hurry, or slur your words and in seconds you can ruin any image of beauty you might have.

It is possible to improve your voice just as you can improve your physical appearance but it will take time. Speech patterns are tenacious—they don't change easily because you learn them when you are young and in an emotional environment. But with motivation and practice, you can change them for the better.

The way to start is to make a tape recording of your voice while you're carrying on a normal conversation. You probably won't believe it's you. That's because you hear yourself partly through bone conduction within your head, which makes your voice sound deeper and more resonant in your own ears. Others hear you through air transmission.

Ideally, a voice should sound natural, sincere, friendly,

and flexible and be free of breathiness or tremolos. Young voices usually have a lighter, younger register than older ones. Older people frequently develop a tremolo and a heaviness to their voices but it needn't be this way. A voice that registers interest, awareness, and zest sheds years.

A quick way to find the best pitch for your voice is to sing a scale—do, re, mi, fa, sol, la, ti, do—beginning as low as you can comfortably sing. The fifth note above this is the point where your voice should sound at its best. Practice speaking at this pitch regularly—recite a poem; make a speech; read a letter aloud—and make every effort to put warmth and tempo into what you say. Tape-record and play back your efforts until you're satisfied. Good breathing is vital. Shallow breathing makes for a wispy voice; breathe deeply from the diaphragm to improve tone quality. Yawn widely a few times to relax your throat and jaw muscles; you'll find that your voice will sound far less tense then. Watch yourself in a mirror as you practice; don't keep your lips tight and flat—this fosters a nasal quality. Instead, keep your lips rounded and speak slowly enough to let good tone and clear enunciation come through.

Watch out for poor speaking habits—slipshod diction can be irritating. So can affectations. Also, try to avoid monotones and mumbling and stumbling through a field of ers, uhs, ahs, and you-knows in every sentence. Careless diction is as unflattering as nasal, raspy, or shrill sounds.

It has been estimated that the average person says about 25,000 words a day. Concentrate on keeping a pleasant tone, clarity, and vitality in your share. You can sound young and alert or old and bored. The choice should be an easy one.

12 / The Way You Dress—Good, Bad, or Indifferent?

At any stage of your life, the clothes you wear can make you and your figure look better or worse. But from the middle years on, it's vital to choose wisely. Pick the right clothes and you can appear more vivacious, shapelier, and younger. Pick the wrong ones and risk looking drab, out-of-shape, and even older than you are.

How do you know what is right and wrong for your to wear? Easy. Whenever you buy anything—a coat, suit, dress, sweater, skirt, or swimsuit—ask yourself (1) Does it flatter my shape, emphasize my good points, and conceal my flaws? (2) Colorwise, does it suit my coloring—my hair, eyes, and complexion? (3) Does it reflect current fashion trends or does it look dated? (4) Do I look and feel better in this particular item of clothing than in any other?

If you hesitate to answer yes to any of these questions, don't make the purchase. If you do, it quite likely will wind up on a hanger at the back of your closet along with your other "mistakes." Like the red miniskirt that looked as though you had borrowed it from a cheerleader. Or the suit jacket edged with fur. The fur encircled your hips and made it seem as though you were wearing a life preserver. And the lime-green evening dress. Whenever you wore it, friends asked if you were feeling ill.

If you're looking for clothes to give a bright confident lift to your appearance, this is a perfect time. It's a time for easy, uncomplicated dressing. Fads no longer dominate the fashion scene. There are still fads, of course. There always will be. But there are so many other fashion choices to make that you can safely let someone else wear the bubble-top blousons, the harem pants, and prairie skirts. The key to smart dressing these days is individuality—which simply means that you make up your own mind about what you wear. You no longer have to play follow-the-leader. What's more, the majority of big name designers are emphasizing simple, fluid lines that have a kind of Peter Pan magic to them. This in itself practically guarantees that you can achieve your goal of dressing youthfully and in good taste. Simplicity is one of the master keys to dressing young. But you don't gain it with exaggerated designs, elaborate materials, and cascades of fringes or ruffles or tiger heads and parrots stenciled on your front or back. You will find it when you choose clothes with clean, uncluttered lines, quality fabrics, and becoming colors.

When You Go Shopping

You probably think <u>you</u> could write the book on clothes shopping—you've done it so often and for so long. But sometimes it's a good idea to review the basic rules.

If you're a dedicated impulse shopper, you probably haven't been paying strict attention to rule one that states: Plan first; shop later.

Let's assume that through magazine, newspaper, television, and radio fashion reporting, you are well aware of the latest trends and styles. And we'll assume, too, that you have sorted through your closets and drawers and have decided what you can salvage from a previous season for this one. (Get rid of anything that's worn, faded, or fits badly so you won't be tempted to "make do" with it). Now comes the important moment: Sit down and make a list of the major purchases you must make in order to have an attractive, suitable, useful wardrobe for the new season. As you prepare your list, group related items. For example, plaid skirt, navy skirt, navy sweater, and white silk blouse. The more mixing and matching you can do, the better. And think color, too, as you plan. Assign two or three basic shades to your "big" purchases such as a coat, suit, or dress. And plan on using brighter accents for small items and accessories.

Stay Away from Memory Lane

You are now ready to go shopping, armed with your season plan and your resolve to avoid temptation. You will not linger at markdown displays. What good is an imported sweater at any price when it has two missing buttons and their nearest replacements are in Paris? And what do you save when you buy a $200 designer dress for $150, then discover it's too long-waisted? Steel yourself, too, against succumbing to sentiment. Don't recall that you had a slithery satin evening skirt when you were eighteen and loved it. The one you want to buy now may be just as slithery but you're not. Remember, your figure has changed and bias skirts aren't for you anymore. And blot out all thoughts about how well certain styles look on your friends. The purple shorts your friend Nancy wore to the picnic last weekend may have looked perky on her; on you they'd show up cellulite.

When you select clothes, take time to try them on. Don't wait to get home, then find out that your purchase was mismarked and that the blouse you wanted to wear that night is two sizes too small. And be sure to study your selections in a good light and from all sides and angles in a three-way mirror. Perfect fit is a must. Don't buy anything that doesn't fit you properly or that cannot be altered to fit correctly. Check to see that fabrics drape gracefully; necklines don't gape; sleeves set right on your shoulders; armholes are comfortable; pleats lie flat; and that waistlines "hit" at your own natural waistline.

If there's a choice, go for quality. You no doubt know from experience that one "good" outfit invariably looks better and outlasts two or three cheaper ones. When buying inexpensive items, always choose the simplest style. Elaborate details have a way of spotlighting poor quality.

And select clothes that fit in with your life-style. If you live in the suburbs, casual, country wear is a logical choice. If you go to an office every day, suits or blouses and skirts may give you the most service. If you have a busy social life, choose basic dresses you can easily dress up with jewelry and other accessories.

Give some thought to where you shop for clothes. Instead of shopping in stores that have replaced salespeople with central checkout counters, more and more women are patronizing small dress shops or boutiques where they can develop a one-to-one relationship with an interested, knowledgeable salesperson. Many of these shops specialize in assembling complete wardrobes for their customers. In other words, they'll take your season plan and work it out with you. It's a nice feeling to get a phone call from a fashion boutique and hear the news that "a beautiful silk suit just came in that is perfect for you. I'm going to hold it until you can come down to look at it." No revolving rack in an impersonal department store can match that for cooperation!

The Importance of Color

Here's a surprise—your favorite color may not be the one that flatters you most. Colors are known to have a strong emotional pull. You may dote on red because it reminds you of your first car. Or blue because someone you admired very much always wore blue. So don't pick your wardrobe colors from the heart; depend on your eyes and a well-lighted mirror to make sure the colors you choose do something for you. Any color you wear should flatter your complexion, your hair, and your eyes.

The skin on your face, neck, arms, and hands will provide the best clues to what colors you should wear. As a rule of thumb, if a color makes your skin look fresh and healthy, wear it. If a color makes your skin look drab and sallow, don't wear it. Experiment until you can tell by looking at a color whether it is right for you. Get some swatches of various colors in a fabric store, bring them home, and hold them up to your face in front of a mirror. You'll see that some make you look washed out; others give you a vibrant, alive look.

If your skin is fair and your hair color light, light or pastel colors with small amounts of stronger, contrasting shades will look well on you.

If your skin is light and your hair color dark, dark or light colors with greater amounts of strongly contrasting color will work well for you.

If your skin is dark and your hair color dark, darker, stronger colors worn with bold contrasts will be a good choice.

Colors Can Change

Don't forget that colors are strongly influenced by light. Whenever you try on a new outfit, make a final check under the light in which you are going to be wearing it. Study the garment in daylight, near a window, or in sunlight to see the full potential of its color.

Colors change in intensity according to fabrics, too. As a rule, they look brightest on hard-surfaced, shiny fabrics and less bright on soft materials with a heavy nap.

Remember also that every color is influenced by the color next to it. If you wear two colors at the same time, one could alter the character of the other. For example, a pale green blouse will look lighter and more yellow against a dark blue skirt, but it will seem darker and more blue when teamed with a yellow skirt.

A Few Specific Color Tips

Black, particularly dull black, reduces the apparent size of a figure. It's not always an easy color to wear because it tends to drain color from the face. But it makes the skin appear clearer and paler. Blue-eyed blondes and brunets, as well as redheads, look well in black.

White increases size, so avoid it if you have a heavy figure. It looks well with all complexions. Blondes look very well in white unless their natural coloring is extremely pale. Redheads wear white well, especially for sports and evening clothes. Dark brunets look best in off-white. It's interesting to note that white combines better with vivid hues than it does with pastels. They tend to make white look dirty.

Green is a cool-looking, sophisticated choice but it can be tricky to wear. Choose carefully from among its wide varieties. Very bright greens drain color from the face; yellow-greens emphasize sallowness; and green in general will make a ruddy complexion look even redder.

Blue is a safe, flattering color. Navy blue makes the skin appear clear and doesn't drain color from the face. It flatters all figure sizes. Soft blues are especially youthful and look equally well on blue-eyed women with blond, dark brown, or black hair. But watch out for intense, brilliant blues—often they can overpower, even making blue eyes seem gray.

Red is a happy, youthful color but not your best choice if yours is a large figure since it tends to increase your size. Most shades of red can be worn successfully with all complexions. Brilliant reds can get tiresome, so watch out and don't overdo red in your wardrobe. When in doubt, use it as an accent.

Brown is a becoming color for most women, especially for sportswear. Redheads and blondes look well in brown; so do light-haired women with brown eyes and fair complexions. However brunets and dark-skinned women should be careful about shades of brown that might intensify the brownish or sallow cast of their complexions. Combining brown with white or bright colors offsets this tendency. In general, beige, the pale member of the brown family, flatters all skin tones. Those with very fair, delicate complexions are the one exception. Beige can make them look washed-out unless it is combined with a contrasting color.

Yellow and oranges are sunny colors that look their best when worn in subdued tints. Natural blondes wear yellow beautifully. Redheads and black-haired women do better if they keep yellow as an accent color. Yellow cannot always be depended upon to flatter a complexion; for example, it's not an ideal choice for a brunet with sallow skin.

Don't Overlook Accessories

By definition an accessory is "an object or device not essential in itself but adding to the beauty, convenience, or effectiveness of something else." Jewelry, scarves, belts, handbags, gloves, even hats and shoes can all be considered accessories. Any one or more of them can transform an ordinary outfit into something very special. The challenge comes in knowing which ones to select and in what colors, materials, and sizes.

Restraint is the word to keep in mind when you shop for accessories. Don't go overboard. If you pick accessories that are too large, too bright, too tiny, too gimmicky, or too anything, your plan to transform a simple costume into a stunning one can meet with disaster.

The logical rule about accessories in general is: Keep them proportionate to your figure. Small woman—small accessories; medium—medium accessories; large—large accessories.

If you're petite, an enormous over-the-shoulder bag and big, chunky jewelry is going to look outlandish on you. A small classic purse and delicate jewelry are for you. If you're very tall or have a large frame, dainty handbags and fragile jewelry are not a wise choice. You're the one who can wear big tote bags and dramatic jewelry with flair.

Accessories can do a lot more than dress up an outfit. Select them with care and you'll discover that they can minimize figure faults. If your neck is short rather than swanlike, don't stress the fact with a large-beaded choker. Choose a graduated string of beads or a trio of long chains to give the illusion of length. Conversely, a thin neck needs large beads worn close to the base of the throat for ultimate flattery.

If you have small hands, don't wear great big rings that look too heavy for your fingers; select rings more in proportion to your delicate hands. Bracelets can be a plus or minus, too. If you have heavy arms and wrists, pass up the cuff bracelets. Choose slender, loose bangles that have an airy look.

More than any other element of clothing, accessories tend to show up as so-called fun wear. Like earrings that light up, handbags that play "I'm in the Money" when opened, gloves with sequined fingernail tips, and T-shirts with cryptic messages stamped on them. The best thing to do about any of these novelty items is to let someone else have the fun. You're striving for a charming, well-groomed, attractive look. Young, yes, but outlandish, never.

Underneath It All

The way undergarments are made today, you'd think they were a second skin. Quicker than you can say "diet and exercise" you can slip into a featherweight wisp of nylon and spandex elastic and find yourself with a firmer, more streamlined silhouette and an inches-smaller waistline. Gone are the old, formidable designs, the heavy materials, and the boning and intricate stitching. Replacing them are stretchy little body slimmers, shapers, smoothers, minimizers, or all-in-ones. Call them what you will, but they do a remarkable job of smoothing out bulges and bumps, all the while letting you feel free and mobile.

If you have a waistline roll, a stomach bulge, fat pads on your hips, or heavy thighs, you'll be pleasantly surprised to discover how much "smooth-power" these airy-looking garments possess. They can have a built-in bra and go from bustline to thighline. Or start at the waistline and have long or short legs. Many have special stretch-lace, or knit or woven panels in strategic places for extra control. If all you need is a little flattening for your stomach, try control-top panty hose. If it's your derriere that's the problem, nylon-spandex elastic panties can lift, define, or flatten. Under clinging clothes, a body stocking will give you minimum but worthwhile all-over firming. And support hose can do nice things for your legs and still look attractively sheer.

If you've been wearing the same bra style and size for longer than you can remember, you're probably missing out on an easy and effective way to improve your silhouette. Breasts change when body weight changes, meaning a new bra size is in order. When you diet, your breasts become smaller along with the rest of you. Conversely, if you gain weight, your bra cup size could increase. And a different style bra may be what you need for a lifted, therefore younger-looking, bustline.

Here's how to find out what size bra you should be wearing. All you need is a tape measure. First, measure around your chest just under your arms. Stand up straight while doing this. If it's an odd number, like 33, go to the next highest even number—in this case, band size 34. Next, measure around the fullest point of your bust across the nipples. (Do this with your bra on.) If this number is one inch more than your band size, your cup size is an *A*. Two inches more than your band size, you're a *B*. Three inches more, you're a *C*. Four inches more, a *D*. Five inches more, a *DD*.

Medical experts say that muscle attachments supporting the breasts need continuing help not to sag. This is especially true as one grows older. So throw out all your old limp, shapeless, faded bras—they're not helping your bustline. And when you shop for a new bra, be sure to get advice first from a salesperson about size and fit. After that, you can go to the self-service racks.

One final word: Bustline, waistline, back, and buttocks make the difference between a matronly figure and a youthful one. If they look good, you look good. So stop and think. If the right bra, body slimmer, power-net panty hose, or control-top panty hose can help firm up, mold, and smooth out one or all of these four key areas and you're not wearing any of them, what are you waiting for?

Shopping for Your Figure Type

IF YOU'RE TALL AND SLENDER. Look for clothes that have a softly tailored look. Avoid too many vertical lines that may exaggerate your height. Round necklines and natural or slightly lower waistlines are your best choice. Blouses and sweaters that contrast with skirts and pants are fine; you're tall enough to carry off such contrasts. You can wear pleated skirts, double-breasted jackets, long sweaters, bulky coats, and wide belts. Choose fabrics with definite body and texture and warm, lively colors. Avoid anything short-waisted; or severe, angular details and too many frills or anything "cute."

IF YOU'RE TALL AND VERY SLIM. You goal is to avoid that beanpole look so pick clothes with soft fullness and fluid movement rather than tight clingy styles. Bloused tops, slightly flared skirts, jackets, or suits with pockets set high on the bodice, and rounded shoulderlines and full sleeves are all becoming to you. You look especially well in big, bulky coats belted at the waist. Fabrics that make others look heavy are ideal for you—shiny satins, metallics, and bulky knits. And you look good in bold prints and large plaids, too.

IF YOU'RE TALL AND FULL-FIGURED. You want clothes to slim your shape, not emphasize it. Tailored styles in low-key colors that stress diagonal or vertical lines are the wisest choice. Stay away from too much trimming. Collarless dresses and coats look well on you. V-necklines are slenderizing; so are straight, easy-fitting skirts with center stitching or a center pleat. Belts? Make yours narrow or medium-wide. Avoid very long or very short jackets and the princess or Empire silhouette. Semifitted styles give you a much beter line. Medium-weight fabrics in medium-size, well-spaced patterns look best on you. Don't pick bulky, shiny, or sheer fabrics or have sharp color contrasts in one outfit. Also taboo: round necklines, large pockets, and dolman sleeves.

IF YOU'RE SHORT AND SLENDER. Simplicity will provide the look you want, meaning understated clothes that don't overpower your figure. Vertical lines will give you height. On the other hand, horizontal lines are out: They can make you look even shorter. One of the prettiest styles for you in both coats and dresses is the fitted, beltless princess style. Round or shallow necklines and short-waisted styles are fine. Match blouses to skirts and pants; keep skirts short and straight or moderately flared. Avoid fussy details, low necklines, and heavy fabrics in loud patterns. Crisp, flat fabrics and small-patterned materials in soft colors are much more flattering.

IF YOU'RE SHORT AND VERY THIN. Play up your petiteness with close-fitting clothes but wear monotones to appear taller. Another way to do this: Stress up-and-down interest whenever possible. Vertical tucks or rows of buttons, for example, are flattering. You're one of the few who can wear ruffles without a worry; but don't overdo it. Have softness in whatever you choose—for example, a chiffon dress with floating panels or a blousy blouse with puffy sleeves and an eyelet trim. All-white outfits are a good choice. Fabrics with body such as tweeds look well on you but avoid overpowering big splash prints and stay with smaller ones. Short jackets, blouses, pants, and bikinis all belong in your wardrobe.

IF YOU'RE SHORT AND PLUMP. When you go shopping, always look for a strong vertical line in whatever you try on. Straight, full-length coats, for example, are a wise choice. Dresses should have a clear vertical line from shoulder to hem; details should attract the eye up and down, never across. Keep skirts slightly flared or straight, with a center closing or pleat. Blouses and sweaters should have center closings as well. Modified V-necklines and natural shoulderlines are becoming. Keep your outfits in one color, preferably dark or muted—strong color contrasts are not for you. Also avoid short or boxy jackets, pleated skirts, wide belts, sleeveless blouses, and dresses. Choose fabrics that are thin or of medium weight with a dull surface, not shy, sheer, clinging fabrics. And knobby, rough fabrics will give you the illusion of added width and weight, so pass them up.

More specifically, if you are small-bosomed with very full hips, remember that emphasis should go above the waist. Your jackets and sweaters should reach no lower than the hipbone. Avoid tight-fitting clothes, particularly pants and skirts.

If you're bosomy with small hips, the opposite is true. In your case, emphasis should go below the waist. When you wear two-color combinations, it's the upper half that should be darker.

If you're both bosomy and full-hipped, de-emphasize your waist. Wear narrow belts and keep accents to a minimum above the waist. Straight-cut pants with a dark jacket is one of your most attractive outfits.

If your figure is rounded and you have a small waist, avoid stressing the curviness, lest you stress the plumpness, too. Wear straight-cut pants and define your waist with tuck-in sweaters and blouses or short jackets.

SKINNY LEGS OR HEAVY LEGS. Not a figure category but many women have the problem and wear the wrong things. For thin legs, choose light stockings, shoes with squared or rounded toes. Avoid shoes and stockings of one color and open-toed shoes. For heavy legs, wear stockings in subdued colors, slightly longer, flared skirts, and untrimmed pumps. Avoid tight, straight skirts and open or strapped shoes.

13/ What's New in Plastic Surgery

Once plastic surgery was the prerogative of a limited number of people. Either they were very rich or they were in the public eye. Also, to have a face lifted, a nose altered, or a chinline improved was considered a very private affair, something like having a social disease or a relative in jail. It simply wasn't discussed.

Times have changed. In the United States each year, more than half a million people undergo cosmetic surgery to improve their looks or to correct congenital or accident-induced physical impairments. They are not all millionaires or in show business and there's nothing hush-hush about it. In fact, cosmetic surgery is as routinely accepted as having braces on one's teeth. Young women feel they no longer have to live with a miserable profile, not when a plastic surgeon can remedy nature's mistake. Parents understand the importance of having their children's facial flaws corrected. Mature women are confidently aware that their sagging jowls, baggy eyes, and face full of loose, wrinkled skin can be eliminated. And it's only fair. As modern medicine lengthens the life span, most people feel physically and mentally vigorous and energetic long after their appearance begins to deteriorate with advancing years.

Here, then, are descriptions of the most common cosmetic procedures, listed generally in the order of popularity, as reported by plastic surgeons.

I'd Like a New Nose

Rhinoplasty is the name given to the operation designed to correct deformities of the nose. Most often the nose is shortened and the hump reduced by removing excess bone and cartilage. Also, the nostrils may be reshaped. The operation takes about one to two hours and the patient usually is up and around the day after surgery, with an average hospital stay of about three days. The normal swelling and discoloration that occurs about the eyes subsides by the end of the first week. A slight swelling of the nose may be present in diminishing amounts for several weeks but most people are able to return to normal activities one or two weeks after the operation.

Usually in a rhinoplasty, all the work is done on the inside of the nose, leaving no scars on the outside. There are exceptions. If it is necessary to make the nostrils smaller, an incision is made where the side of the nostril adjoins the upper lip. Because this is located in a natural body fold, the scar is practically invisible within a few weeks.

Most individuals have a rhinoplasty to improve their appearance although some older people find it the solution for breathing difficulties that cause severe headaches and sinus trouble. Some of the limiting factors a surgeon must consider are the contour and shape of the face, the texture and thickness of the skin, the healing powers of the tissues, and the position of the chin, lip, and forehead as well as the depth of angle between the forehead and nose. Candidates for a rhinoplasty must remember that the surgical goal is improvement—the achievement of better facial harmony. It is not geared to fulfill one's fantasies about a pert, retroussé nose, or a Barrymore profile.

Open Up Your Eyes

Blepharoplasty is the unwieldy name for a form of plastic surgery that's increasingly popular these days, especially among mature women. They may or may not be able to pronounce the term but they know it means getting rid of those sagging, baggy eyelids that occur, thanks to a combination of hereditary and aging factors.

The operation may be done separately or in conjunction with a face-lift. Both upper and lower lids usually are corrected at the same time. Incisions are made in the fold of the upper lid and just below the eyelashes of the lower lid. Then those unwanted little pouches of fat and the excess skin are removed and the incisions are very delicately stitched closed. The operation usually lasts one or two hours. As a rule, there is little or no pain in the postoperative period. Swelling and discoloration usually subside within ten days. By this time, the thread-thin scars can be camouflaged successfully by makeup. After a few months they almost disappear. In fact, no one would suspect that you have had a blepharoplasty except upon close scrutiny. And sufficient mascara can put a stop to that.

Several weeks after the lower lid correction, the surgeon may suggest a light chemical peeling that can produce further tightening of the skin.

Eyebrows Get a Lift, Too

The eyebrow lift can be combined with surgery to eliminate sagging eyelids, done in conjunction with a face-lift or performed as an independent procedure. When the outer ends of the eyebrows droop noticeably, it causes the upper eyelids to bulge and descend until they seem to lie on the eyelashes. Excising the skin just above the drooping section of the brow or at the hairline, thereby lifting the outer end of the eye structure or area does away with this unattractive condition. The eyes appear much larger and more youthful and there's a definite lessening of the "crow's feet" so often found next to the outer corners of the eyes.

About Face-lifts

It's called a *rhytidectomy* but most women who have had this surgery call it a new lease on life. What it does is diminish the conspicuous marks of aging—the excessive wrinkling and overstretched skin folds, the pouches along the jawline, and the "tired look" that degenerative changes have brought to the outer layer of the skin.

Generally, a face-lift can be divided into three parts: the neck lift, the cheek lift, and the temporal, or brow lift. In some patients, it may be necessary to perform a fourth operation to remove excessive fat under the chin. Not every patient requires all four.

The operation may be performed in a hospital or in an outpatient surgical clinic. Not everyone is an acceptable candidate. Surgery is not advised for persons with serious diseases, those who are too obese, or for those who have unrealistic expectations from the surgery or the wrong motivations.

Face-lift incisions usually are made in front of and behind the ear, placed in the natural creases of the skin and in the hair-bearing areas of the scalp in order to camouflage scars. The skin is separated from the underlying tissues and rotated or stretched to take up any slack. The excessive skin is removed and the remaining skin then sutured back into place. Following surgery, generally a firm wraparound facial dressing is worn around the face and neck for a day or so. Swelling and discoloration, usually not painful, will generally subside in a week to ten days. Scars will be hidden in the hair or in natural facial folds, eventually to become virtually undetectable. Soon after the operation, you can count on cosmetics and the right hair styling to help hide the scars.

How Long Will It Last

All women contemplating a face-lift want to know how much improvement to expect and how long it will last. Improvement depends upon the degree and amount of wrinkling. If it is marked, results may be dramatic. If sagging occurs at a young age and the operation is done to keep the patient looking young, improvement may be subtle.

How long the improvement will last cannot be accurately predicted. It largely depends upon the aging rate of each individual. If the wrinkling was originally severe, it obviously will take longer for the condition to reappear. Ideally, improvement lasts from five to ten years. If and when the facial skin does begin to sag again, a less involved and highly effective secondary "tuck-up" may be performed. Incisions and scars are basically located as they were originally. The recovery period is shorter. In fact, the surgery can be performed periodically, often on an outpatient basis, or as a one-day hospital procedure.

Improvement with the "tuck-up" operation is usually quite dramatic. Original face-lift surgery sets up conditions that enhance circulatory efficiency, create a neater fit because of less stretching, and bring about reciprocal support and reinforcement produced by the second lifting of the skin. The procedure is particularly advantageous for patients who undergo the primary face-lift at a relatively young age. It sets the stage for a continuing maintenance program that keeps the individual looking as well as possible for the remainder of her life. For older patients, the "tuck-up" provides the chance to achieve a higher degree of improvement.

There's one more comment about rhytidectomy—results are short-lived on a heavy face. So if you're overweight and contemplating a face-lift, first go on a diet.

Getting Your Ears Pinned Back

Cosmetic surgery follows current fashions closely, according to one plastic surgeon. He has noticed that when hairstyles shorten, a spurt of women patients come in to have their protruding ears fixed. The operation is called *otoplasty* and it is designed to correct deformed and flattened as well as protruding ears. It may be done by means of incisions on the front surface of the ear, or behind the ear, to reshape the cartilage. Earlobes get larger with age; they can be trimmed down to a smaller size during the operation.

You're out of the hospital as soon as twenty-four hours after surgery. A bandage is worn over the ears for about one week; then it is worn for several more weeks at night to provide protection while you sleep. Scars are usually inconspicuous because they lie in the ear's natural creases. Some of the most satisfied patients are those who have had their protruding ears corrected in adult life after years of "hiding" them.

Breast Correction

There's *mammaplasty*, or breast reduction and *mastoplasty* or breast augmentation and still more as far as breast surgery goes. Plastic surgeons now can not only reduce or increase breast size but they can improve the shape of breasts and correct mismatched breasts. And for cancer patients who have had a mastectomy or breast removal, they can reconstruct a breast.

Breast reductions are usually long procedures that can take four or five hours to perform and require about ten days of hospitalization for recovery purposes.

Breast augmentation is simpler. It requires approximately a two-hour operation and about a week's hospitalization.

Most patients who have had a mastectomy have reconstruction after the area has healed. And many women who had mastectomies years ago are having reconstruction done today. There is a new trend, however. Mastectomy and reconstruction procedures are now being done in one operation with the plastic surgeon working with the cancer surgeon.

Implant devices used in breast augmentation or reconstruction are much improved. Often breast-shaped envelopes of clear plastic, filled with liquid silicone and saline solutions are used. Inside the flesh, they have the weight and feel of living tissue. A new type of implant, designed for softer, more natural breasts, has an inner pocket containing liquid silicone and an outer envelope surrounding it that is filled with a salt solution. Operative techniques, too, are vastly improved. Surgeons are skilled at locating scars so that they can be easily covered, even by a bikini top.

Body Contour Surgery

Don't think that cosmetic operations to improve the figure stop with the breasts. When diet and exercise fail to accomplish it, plastic surgery can remove excess fat in various parts of the body and tighten up and lift loose flabby skin here and there. Jodhpur thighs, saddlebag hips, flaps of skin that hang like an apron on the abdomen, hanging folds on upper arms, sagging buttocks, and loose skin on inner legs—all yield to the plastic surgeon's art. Body contour operations may be long— some combinations take up to six hours—and hospitalization ranges from several days to two weeks but for the patient who faces the world with a new, more streamlined silhouette and a body that's much more comfortable to live with, it's all worthwhile.

How to Locate a Plastic Surgeon

Before you start looking for a plastic surgeon, you should realize that not every plastic surgeon performs every type of plastic surgery. It's a field with many divisions. The general categories are as follows:

GENERAL PLASTIC SURGEONS. These are the general practitioners of plastic surgery in that they operate on all parts of the body. Not all plastic surgeons do cosmetic surgery. Some perform reconstructive surgery only. Many do both. Others may limit themselves to cosmetic surgery of the face alone. Or to the entire body.

HEAD AND NECK SURGEONS (OTOLARYNGOLOGISTS). Specialists in the head and neck area. Some do cosmetic facial surgery only. Others do both cosmetic and reconstructive surgery in this region of the body.

EYE SURGEONS (OPTHALMOLOGISTS). They do cosmetic and reconstructive surgery about the eyes. Very few limit themselves to cosmetic surgery alone.

SKIN SURGEONS (DERMATOLOGISTS). They mostly do skin sanding, hair transplants, and removal of small new growths. Some do skin surgery of the eyelids and other types of cosmetic surgery of the face.

A good place to start your search for a plastic surgeon is at your own family physician's office. He or she should be able to evaluate what you want done and refer you to the most highly qualified plastic surgeon or dermatologist in your area.

Or your local county medical society should be able to give you names of active cosmetic facial surgeons.

Get a copy of the *Directory of Medical Specialists,* usually available in medical as well as some public libraries. There you will be able to check the credentials of your local plastic surgeons, head and neck, and eye and skin surgeons. Find out if they are members of the American Academy of Facial Plastic and Reconstructive Surgery, the American Association of Cosmetic Surgeons, the American Society of Aesthetic Plastic Surgery, the American Society of Opthalmic Plastic and Reconstructive Surgery, or the American Society for Dermatologic Surgery. You can write to any of these organizations and ask for a list of names of member surgeons in your area.

Finally, ask friends and relatives who have had plastic surgery to tell you about their experiences.

Now, armed with a list of surgeons in your community who perform the type of plastic surgery you're seeking, make appointments with the two or three whose names appear most frequently on your checklist.

Evaluating the Surgeon

When you arrive for a consultation, note whether the office staff is friendly and helpful. This is important because you'll be in close contact with these people during and after your operation.

Keep in mind that a good surgeon will take a personal interest in you, your health, and your safety. He will not rush to sign you up for an operation. He'll take time to get a thorough medical history from you and satisfy himself that you are physically and emotionally fit to undergo the surgery you want. He'll also want to make sure that your motivations are good, your expectations realistic, and that you will not be adversely affected in any way.

Be suspicious of a doctor who makes flamboyant claims or assures you that "you're going to look marvelous after your face-lift." A qualified surgeon will explain the operation you're going to have and tell you just what you can expect before, during, and after. He'll document your case with photographs and he'll also discuss his fees with you in advance. He'll make no outlandish guarantees.

Prices are competitive in plastic surgery, as in other fields. And as with any service, surgery included, you get what you pay for. If the fees quoted seem unusually low in comparison with those commonly charged in your community, think twice. Also, since cosmetic surgery is an elective procedure, it's up to you to decide when is the best time for your operation.

According to the American Academy of Facial Plastic and Reconstructive Surgery, Inc., who provided most of the information in this chapter, even with good word-of-mouth recommendations, you should consult at least three certified plastic surgeons before making a final choice. Having three or more consultations will cost more, they say, but it may save you heartache and additional expense in repairing surgery that was not right for you.

One final note: If you are having facial surgery, arrange to see a hairdresser and a makeup specialist just as soon as your doctor says you may. The hairdresser can advise you regarding a becoming new hairstyle, and the makeup expert can show you how to apply your cosmetics so that they do the most for your new look. Psychologically, it will be an important boost for you, too.

14 / Your Personal Beauty and Health Plan

Make the Most of Your Looks

1. Don't go without makeup; realize how becoming a touch of mascara, blusher, and lipstick can be.
2. Give your skin the moisturizing it needs to keep it looking fresh and revitalized. Remember, wrinkles are less noticed when your complexion is clear and dewy-looking.
3. Keep your hair gleaming and your scalp healthy with frequent shampoos and conditioning. Have your hair cut in a flattering, up-to-date style and take advantage of hair color and perms to keep it looking its best.
4. Be fastidious about your person; use deodorants and depilatories regularly. Don't always rush through a bath or shower; make a beauty occasion of them at least once a week—use a body moisturizer and give yourself a facial or some other pampering skin treatment.
5. Remember your hands are always on display.

Keep them perfectly groomed; that means hand creams or lotions and weekly manicures.

6. Don't skip dental appointments. An attractive smile is a beauty plus and you won't have one if your teeth are neglected.

7. The same holds true for eye checkups. And be sure to select glasses in a shape and color that are flattering to your face.

8. Keep up with new makeup trends and techniques; you can date yourself if you stay with the old ways all the time.

Make the Most of Your Figure

1. Be absolutely honest with yourself about the shape you're in. Don't ignore your body; study it and plan how to improve it.

2. Diet if you must; don't postpone it. But stay with a sensible diet based on sound nutrition and lose slowly; crash diets do more harm than good.

3. Think "good posture" at all times; don't give in to slouching and slumping. Whether standing, sitting, or moving about, keep your head lifted, your shoulders back, and your midriff tightened.

4. Walk with a lively, energetic step.

5. Put together an exercise program for yourself—it can be something as simple as arm stretches, torso twists, and toe touches—but make it a daily part of your life.

6. Whenever you can, walk. A jogging or running routine may be difficult for you to maintain but you can always walk, so just don't sit there.

7. Get sufficient rest; no one looks younger when she's yawning.

8. Have regular physical checkups.

Make the Most of Your Clothes

1. Never wear anything that calls attention to itself, not to you.
2. Choose clothes that suit your figure and your way of life and go for quality rather than quantity.
3. Figure out the colors that flatter you the most and build your wardrobe around them.
4. Know your best points and use clothes to dramatize them—V-necked blouses for a pretty throat; wide belts for a narrow waistline; smart shoes for good-looking legs.
5. Choose imaginative accessories—scarfs, jewelry, handbags, and so forth—but keep them harmonious and in good taste. Fads and novelties are out.
6. Don't buy hit-or-miss; select everything you buy in relation to what you already have in your closet or with a specific ensemble in mind.
7. Be sure all your clothes fit properly: sleeves that are too long or too short, a bunchy waistline, or a gaping neckline can ruin your appearance.
8. Keep everything you wear in perfect condition—cleaned and pressed with no missing buttons, rips, frays, or pinned-up hems.
9. Wear a properly fitting bra and if you need one, a body-shaper, to make your figure trimmer so that your clothes look their best on you.

Make the Most of Your Personality

1. Develop your own individual qualities; don't be a carbon copy of someone else.
2. Be interested in everyone and everything.
3. Be as good a listener as you are a talker.
4. Keep your voice pleasantly modulated, soft and sincere rather than strident.

5. Avoid quarrels, arguments, and tears—they'll make no positive contribution to your life.
6. Make new friends; associate with young people.
7. Continue to develop new interests and new hobbies.
8. Choose perfumes you like and wear them all the time so that they become part of you. A fragrant aura is the right companion for a pleasing personality.
9. Smile; don't frown at the world.

ABOUT THE AUTHOR

Kay Sullivan's editorial career has been diverse. She has been a beauty, a fashion and an entertainment editor on national publications. Most recently as head of *Redbook*'s Special Interest Publications, she planned and edited magazines on a variety of subjects, including decorating, food, flowers and plants, baths and kitchens, and child care. One of her most successful introductions was the popular "*Redbook's* Be Beautiful."